THE MEDIEVAL LIBRARY UNDER
THE GENERAL EDITORSHIP OF
SIR ISRAEL GOLLANCZ, Litt.D., F.B.A.

King Alfreds Jewel found
in the Isle of Athelney now
in the Ashmolean Museum,
Oxford.

ASSER'S LIFE OF KING ALFRED : TRANSLATED WITH INTRODUCTION AND NOTES BY L. C. JANE, M.A.

COOPER SQUARE PUBLISHERS, INC.
NEW YORK
1966

Published 1966 by Cooper Square Publishers, Inc.
59 Fourth Avenue, New York, N. Y. 10003
Library of Congress Catalog Card No. 66-27658

Printed in the United States of America
by Noble Offset Printers, Inc., New York, N. Y. 10003

"ALFRED, ENGLAND'S HEARDMAN, ENGLAND'S DARLING."

"HE WAS KING OF ENGLAND: HE TAUGHT THEM
THAT COULD HEAR HIM, HOW THEY SHOULD LEAD THEIR LIVES."

"ALFRED WAS A KING OF ENGLAND, THAT WAS VERY STRONG."

"HE WAS BOTH A KING AND A SCHOLAR: HE LOVED WELL GOD'S
WORK."

"HE WAS WISE, AND ADVISED OF HIS TALK."

"HE WAS THE WISEST MAN THAT WAS IN ALL ENGLAND."

'The Proverbs of Alfred,' Sir John Spelman,
Life of King Ælfred the Great, p. 129.

INTRODUCTION

Across the stage of history the Anglo-Saxon kings and statesmen move in somewhat shadowy procession. Most of them are little more than names to us, some of them are rather less, and even in the case of the best-known figures, it is difficult, if not impossible, to form any clear conception of their personality. Very little enthusiasm is aroused in this twentieth century by the memory of Athelstan, under whom the political power of the Saxon monarchy perhaps attained its zenith; or by that of Dunstan, first of the statesmen-prelates of our history, or of Godwine, his secular counterpart. We are not quite sure, and most of us care less, whether the first of these did in truth cause "his brother Edwin to be drowned in the sea"; or whether the second did or did not display considerable mechanical skill at the Witenagemot of Calne; or whether the third was or was not an accessory before the fact to the murder of the son of Ethelred the Unready. But to this general indifference there is one noteworthy exception, and though more than a thousand years have passed since his death, the name of Alfred still strikes a chord in the heart of every Englishman.

We are indeed forced, in the light of historical criticism, to admit that he did not accomplish all that has been claimed for him ; many of the stories associated with his name have been relegated to the domain of fiction. We are no longer permitted to believe that he founded our navy and reformed a University, that he divided his kingdom into shires and originated our legal system, or that he burned cakes in Somersetshire and posed as an itinerant musician in Wiltshire. There is even a tendency to share the scepticism of Gibbon as to his mission to India. But while the Alfred myth must take its place beside those of Arthur and Charlemagne, there has been no decrease in that admiration for the king's work which long since earned for him the title of " The Great," or in that high estimate of his character which is expressed in the epithet, " The Truth-teller." He is still the best beloved of English kings ; we can still echo the sentiment of a great novelist that " one can only honour and love his memory." That memory has, perhaps, rather gained than lost by the better understanding of what the man really did and of what he really was. Our admiration for him is hardly lessened because we know that when all things were most hopeless, he did not " abandon all his warriors " and burn cakes in a cowherd's hovel, or because we realise that his final victory was probably the result not of a miracle or of good luck, but of organisation and forethought. Alfred's memory has gained by the triumph of the truth that he loved so well. When the mass of tradition has been swept away, his greatness is the more evident.

Yet, despite the fact that this greatness cannot be doubted, it is a little hard, after the lapse of a thousand years, to realise how much he did, and it is questionable whether the mere record of his achievements as the saviour of the nascent civilisation of England and the regenerator of his kingdom would in itself have sufficed to do more than to lead us to respect his memory. That Alfred is not a mere shadow, that he is a man, that we have for his memory the deeper feeling of affection, must be attributed to the fact that his personality yet lives. That his personality does live is due in no small measure to his own writings, to the accidental self-revelation found in them. In the prefaces to the translations which he made or caused to be made, and in those translations themselves, which are so much more than mere renderings of Latin into Anglo-Saxon, we find many sidelights on his character and mode of thought. We find enough material here, perhaps, to enable us to form a fairly adequate conception of Alfred.

But at the same time it is to another source that we must turn for the details which fill in the picture, and even for the means to read aright the hints which are contained in the king's own works. If it were not for his biographer, we should be driven to rely very largely on conjecture where at present we have definite information. We should know but little of his private life, and we should in all probability miss many points in his character. Asser has given us not a mere chronicle of the reign but a picture of Alfred the man, and for that reason we may pass over his faults of style and method, we may pardon his many deficiencies, and we may feel no little gratitude to him. Indeed, as long as the memory of the king is treasured, the name of his biographer should at least be remembered.

The Author. Beyond the information contained in the present work, we know practically nothing of the life of Asser; only a few additional details are to be derived from the casual notices of other writers and from the charters of the period. Neither the date nor the place of his birth are recorded, but he was a native of Wales, and was brought up and educated at St. David's—Nobis, who held that see from 840 to 873, being related to him. At the same place he received the tonsure, and, in due course, was ordained. His life was not wholly peaceful. Hemeid, King of Dyfed, was at this time making frequent attacks upon the Church of St. David's, and the clergy were forced on several occasions to abandon their home. Asser seems to have shared the exile of his relative, the bishop; in any case he was once driven from St. David's. But he returned, and would appear to have acquired a position of considerable importance. For, when he was invited to enter the service of Alfred, he felt constrained to consult

" his people " before concluding any definite agreement, while the king, on his side, offered liberal compensation to the Welshman for the sacrifice which he was asked to make. It is impossible to say with certainty what the actual position of Asser was; as will be seen later, it has been suggested that he was Bishop of St. David's.

As soon as the immediate peril from the Danes had been removed, Alfred began the work of educating his people and himself. But the supply of teachers in his own dominions was inadequate, and he was therefore compelled to invite the assistance of foreign scholars. Among those so invited was Asser, to whom the king sent an embassy, which served to guide him on the lengthy journey from St. David's to the royal court. It was in or about the year 884 that our author first came into contact with Alfred; the confused arrangement of the *Life* prevents us from assigning any more definite date. Passing through " vast tracts of country," Asser eventually found the king at Dean in Sussex, and was cordially received by him. Alfred would appear to have been very favourably impressed by the Welshman, for he urged him to take up his residence at his court. Asser refused to do so, on the ground that his duty to the Church and people of St. David's forbade it ; nor would he consent to remain even for part of each year in Wessex without previous consultation with his people. As he found, however, that the king was extremely anxious to secure his services, he

undertook eventually to consult his friends and return with
a definite answer at the end of six months. Accordingly,
after having spent four days at the court, he set out on his
homeward journey.

He had reached Winchester when he was struck down
with fever, and though he succeeded in making his way
back to Wales, he lingered between life and death for
" twelve months and a week." Alfred, who had heard
nothing of his illness, was much concerned at the failure
of Asser to return at the appointed time, and sent letters
to him asking for the reason, to which our author replied
that he would certainly return to Wessex if his life were
spared.

Meanwhile he had discussed the royal proposals with
his people, and on their advice had decided to devote half
his time to the service of Alfred. This decision was
brought about by the political condition of South Wales.
Hemeid of Dyfed would appear to have had a particular
antipathy for the Church of St. David's; certainly he
did much damage to it, and the clergy were ardently desirous of finding some release from his constant attacks.
In the proposed connection between Asser and Alfred a
way of escape seemed to offer itself. Many of the Welsh
princes, in their desire to avoid subjection to the sons of
Rhodri Mawr or to the ealdorman of Mercia, had placed
themselves under the suzerainty of Wessex, and among
their number was Hemeid. The clergy of St. David's

therefore hoped that if Asser were to become a friend of
Alfred, he might be able to influence the king to inter-
vene and to check the depredations of Hemeid. Accordingly they consented to the partial residence of Asser in
Wessex, and it was arranged that he should spend six
months in each country, residing either six months con-
secutively at the court, or else dividing that period into
two parts, so that he "should dwell for three months in
Britain and for three months in the land of the Saxons."

With this answer Asser returned to the king after a
lapse of over a year from his first visit. On this occasion
he found Alfred at Leonaford, and was received with un-
abated cordiality. He at once began to assist the king in
his studies, and, it may be presumed, to advance the in-
terests of St. David's. According to his own account,
he read to the king "whatsoever books he would and
which we had at hand." In this way eight months were
passed, the king refusing his teacher leave to return home,
until at last Asser began to doubt whether he would ever
be allowed to go back to Wales.

He had, in fact, resolved to demand permission when
on Christmas Eve, at dusk, he was summoned to the
royal presence. The king then gave him the two monasteries of Congresbury and Banwell, "with all that was in
them," in addition to a silken pall and "as much incense
as could be borne by a strong man." He added that
these presents were merely an earnest of future favours,

and allowed him to "ride to those two monasteries" at once.

In the year 887, Asser was responsible for leading Alfred to undertake both the compilation of his "Hand-book" and the work of translating from Latin into Anglo-Saxon. He tells us that one day he happened to quote a passage which made so great an impression on the king that he wished to have it written in the book of private devotions which he constantly carried about with him. This book was, however, already filled, and Asser suggested that the quotation should be written on a separate sheet, as then, if other suitable passages were discovered, they might be collected together. Alfred agreed to this suggestion, and in the course of time the book grew until it reached the size of a Psalter. The king kept it constantly by him, and called it his "Enchiridion," or "Handbook." The compilation of this collection of favourite passages had another result, for it led Alfred to wish to translate them for the benefit of his subjects, and may thus be regarded as the origin of his various translations.

William of Malmesbury tells us that Asser also produced a simplified Latin version of *Boethius*, from which Alfred made his translation, "a labour in those days needful, in ours absurd." There is nothing inherently improbable in this story, but the expression used by our author in describing Werferth's version of Gregory's

Dialogues may possibly have suggested the idea of a simplified text to Malmesbury. On the other hand, in his preface to Gregory's *Pastoral Care*, Alfred says, " I began to translate into English the book which is called in Latin *Pastoralis*, and in English *Shepherd's Book*, sometimes word by word, and sometimes according to the sense, as I learnt it from Plegmund my archbishop, and Asser my bishop, and Grimbold my mass-priest, and John my mass-priest." This seems rather to lend colour to the story in Malmesbury.

At a date subsequent to his first visit, but otherwise uncertain, Alfred presented Asser with the whole diocese of Exeter in the land of the Saxons and in Cornwall. Our author gives us no further information about himself.

But, from the notice of his death in the *Chronicle*, and from the old episcopal lists, we find that he was subsequently Bishop of Sherborne, and it has been suggested that he then settled permanently in Wessex. We find him witnessing various charters of Edward the Elder in 901, 903 and 904, though the authenticity of the texts is open to question. Another charter purports to record an exchange effected between Edward and Asser, the latter of whom received lands at Wellington, West Buckland and Bishop's Lydeard, Somerset, in return for handing over to the king the monastery of Plympton in Devonshire. The death of Asser is recorded under 906 in the *Brut y Tywysogion*, under 908 in the *Annales*

Cambriæ, and under 910 in the *Chronicle*. Florence of Worcester is clearly in error in placing his death in 883.

In addition to the ascertained facts as to the life of Asser, certain conjectures have been put forward. Ingulf says that he was Abbot of Bangor, but there is, of course, no sort of authority for this statement. On the other hand, much may be said for the theory that he was Bishop of St. David's, a position which is assigned to him by Giraldus Cambrensis. Neither of the two objections which have been urged against this statement would appear to be conclusive. The first is that his name does not occur in the lists of bishops, but it is admitted that those lists are defective. The second is based on the fact that Alfred calls him " my bishop" in his preface to the *Pastoral Care* ; it is said that the expression "my " would not have been used if Asser had held a Welsh see. On the other hand, as Plummer has pointed out, the position held by our author at Alfred's court, or the fact that the princes of South Wales had accepted the suzerainty of Wessex, might account for the use of the term. In any case, it is clear that Asser cannot be here called " my bishop" in respect of the see of Sherborne, since the preface is addressed to Wulfsige, who was in possession of that see. The supposition that Asser was Bishop of St. David's would therefore remove a difficulty. There are, perhaps, additional arguments in favour of the theory. As has been pointed out already, he would appear to have

held a position of some considerable importance at St.
David's, and the phrase "my people," which he uses in
connection with the clergy of that place, would seem to
suggest episcopal rank.   Finally, in describing the attacks
of Hemeid on St. David's, Asser uses the term "antistes,"
which may mean "bishops" as well as "clergy," and
includes Nobis and himself among their number.   Taken
in its context, the translation "bishops" is possibly the
more probable, and thus our author may himself state by
implication that he held the see of St. David's; but the
evidence on either side is too meagre to justify definite
assertion.

A further difficulty arises in the matter of the grant of
Exeter.   Asser uses the word "parochia," which in most
cases means the jurisdiction of a bishop.   There was,
however, no diocese of Exeter until the time of Edward
the Confessor.   It has been suggested by Plummer that
"Alfred may have wished to place the districts round
Exeter under episcopal supervision without necessarily
intending to create a definite diocese."   Asser might have
then succeeded to the whole see of Sherborne, to which
Devon and Cornwall normally belonged, on the death of
Wulfsige.   Or it is perhaps possible that Asser was made
Bishop of Cornwall, which district would seem to have
had an intermittent and irregular succession of prelates,
being at times attached to Sherborne, and at times
apparently distinct.

There is a story, which is quoted by Leland from a lost life of St. Grimbald, to the effect that Asser was sent to the continent to conduct that scholar to the West Saxon court. In the text of the *Life of Alfred*, we find that the King "sent messengers into Gaul to fetch masters, and summoned thence Grimbald." But it is impossible to say definitely whether Asser was or was not one of these envoys. The fact that he uses Frankish expressions, and that his description of the situation of Paris would seem to be drawn from personal knowledge, has been urged in favour of accepting the story; but the intercourse between England and the continent, so frequent during Alfred's reign, might account for the Frankish influence in Asser, and the description of Paris may well have been taken from a native of that city. The fact that Asser does not say that he went to fetch Grimbald is a strong argument against the truth of the story, since elsewhere he does not display any undue modesty. On the contrary, he is very fond of telling us that he has seen such a place or such a person. On the whole, then, the balance of probability would appear to be against the view that Asser was one of the messengers sent to fetch Grimbald.

Beyond the present work there are no extant writings of Asser. The so-called *Annales Asserii*, or *Annals of St. Neot*, are a compilation from various sources dating from the eleventh or twelfth century. They have no connection whatever with our author except that the compiler made use of the *Life of Alfred*. Giraldus Cambrensis, if he were indeed the author of the *Vita Sancti Ethelberti* which has come down to us, mentions Asser as his authority for saying that Offa ordered an enquiry into the miracles of the saint, and if this be so, then the quotation must be from some lost work. But it may be mentioned that the identity of the *Vita S. Ethelberti*, which is preserved by Bromton, with that of Giraldus, is itself doubtful. Bale and Pitts attributed other works to Asser, but there is no evidence of their existence; and in one case, that of the *Enchiridion*, the allusion is clearly to the " Handbook " of the text, which was not really the production of our author.

The Life of Alfred. It has been contended that the *Life of Alfred* is not in reality the work of Asser, but a forgery of the tenth or eleventh century, produced by a monk of St. Neot's. Mr. Stevenson, however, in his edition of the book, has conclusively shown that the attack on the authenticity of Asser rests either on the many interpolated passages or on misunderstandings. The latter can easily arise from the confused style of the author, from the frequently corrupt state even of the genuine portion of the book, and from the lack of any clear arrangement. The *Life of Alfred* is, then, a contemporary account of the king by one who knew him well, though, as will appear later, it is by no means easy to separate the genuine text from the mass of interpolated matter.

The date of the composition of the *Life* is fixed by a statement in the text. Asser tells us that he was writing in the forty-fifth year of Alfred's life, and as he has already given us the year 849 as the date of the king's birth, it follows that the second date must be 893-894. In addition to this definite statement, there is much evidence in the text that Alfred was still alive, since he is constantly alluded to in the present tense. The work is incomplete, as we have it, either because it was never finished, or because some part of it has been lost. The chronicle of events does not extend beyond the year 888, and the book ends abruptly after an account of the way in which Alfred's judges devoted themselves to the task of learning to read.

As has been hinted already, the *Life* consists of two parts. On the one hand we have a series of annals extending from the year of Alfred's birth to 888, and containing much material which is only very indirectly concerned with the life of the king. On the other hand we have, interspersed among the annals, a number of biographical passages. The source of the annalistic portion of the book is clearly some version of the *Chronicle*, as is shown by the fact that the language of the present work is often practically identical with that of the *Chronicle* as we have it, while in places Asser falls into error owing to his imperfect knowledge of Anglo-Saxon. But he often adds pieces of information, and constantly adapts his narrative for the benefit of Welsh readers. On occasion he possibly gives a more accurate account than does the *Chronicle*. The biographical details cannot be traced to any known source, and must be regarded as the author's original contribution.

It has sometimes been suggested that the *Life* as we have it is a combination of two distinct works, and even that it is the production of two different persons. The duality of authorship, however, can hardly be admitted in view of the fact that the same peculiar uses of words are found in both sections of the work. There is also a noteworthy similarity of phraseology in places, and the difference in style is no greater than might be naturally expected. Nor can the annalistic portion be regarded as a later addition. In passing from the annals to biographical matter, Asser more than once states that he is now turning from a mere chronicle of events to his true subject, the life and character of Alfred. Such a statement would hardly have appeared if the annals and the biography had been separately prepared. Still more conclusive is the passage where the author states that it is his intention to " set forth what little has come to his knowledge " concerning the life and manners of Alfred, and also to " tell not a little of the deeds which he wrought." The latter phrase can hardly refer to anything but the annalistic portion of the work, since it will be noticed that a contrast is drawn between the " life " and the " deeds " of the king. It must therefore be regarded as established that Asser adopted this curious form for his book, making it an ill-arranged combination of general annals and personal details. The method is peculiar, but Mr. Stevenson has pointed out that there are parallels in Frankish biographies. In some respects the system adopted is not unlike that of Jocelin of Brakelond, who adds to his portraiture of Abbot Samson details as to the general history of St. Edmundsbury.

The confusion which is caused by this mixture of chronicle and biography is increased by Asser's lack of method. It is possible that a displacement of the sheets in the lost MS. may account for something, but it is no doubt true that the author was not skilled in arranging his materials. Indeed their arrangement, or rather lack of arrangement, might almost give rise to the supposition that the work was never revised with a view to "publication." Instances of the confusion of the text abound. In the account of Alfred's illnesses it is almost hopeless, if indeed much of that passage is not really an interpolation. Again, in the famous story of the book, if the order in the text represents the order of events, we are asked to believe that Alfred was an expert hunter at the tender age of four years. In his account of the scholars brought into England by the king, we are left in doubt as to whether Asser was the last to arrive or no, as well as to the date to which his coming is to be assigned. It is in fact clear that no regard is paid in the *Life* to strict chronology, and it would be unsafe to base any argument on the mere order of the text. This is illustrated by the fact that after he has carried the annals down to the year 884, Asser suddenly turns back to the events of 868.

In the matter of style, the *Life* is almost equally disappointing, and we may regret that Alfred was not fortunate enough to find a biographer who could do real justice to his subject. Asser's sentences are often extremely long and so involved as to be very hard to understand, and this difficulty is increased by his excessive partiality for parentheses. His casual use of conjunctions is a marked feature of his writing and is sometimes a source of further trouble. To take but one example of his carelessness in this respect: after describing the way in which the education of Alfred was neglected in his childhood, and recording his skill in hunting, Asser introduces the story of the book with an "ergo." He is often rather florid, as for example in the similes with which he occasionally begins the biographical passages; and he is partial to redundant phrases. He has a habit of repeating both expressions and short passages, and this habit is so marked as almost to suggest that he was not quite at his ease when writing in Latin. On the other hand, he does occasionally rise to a comparatively high level, as for example in the passage in which he compare Alfred's search for learning to a bee's search for honey.

But the style of Asser, taken as a whole, leaves a great deal to be desired.

There are comparatively few quotations in the *Life*, and those which do occur are not calculated to create a very favourable opinion of the extent of the author's learning. He misunderstands the passage from Sedulius which he inserts in the genealogy of Alfred, confusing the comic character Geta with the god Geata. He quotes incorrectly from the *Pastoral Care* of Gregory, but in this case he would appear to have been relying either on his memory or on a paraphrase, since he gives the sense of the passage. In quoting from St. Augustine, he falls into two errors; he says that he is quoting the Bible, and he does not give the words of his author accurately. It may be noted that the biblical quotations are unusually few in number.

From Einhard's *Vita Caroli Magni*, Asser borrows without acknowledgment, and it would seem that, to some extent at least, his work was modelled on that of the biographer of the great emperor. It has been suggested that to this fact the absence of any description of the personal appearance of Alfred may be traced. Einhard postpones his portrait of his hero until the end of his book, and it may be that our author intended to conclude in a similar manner, but for some reason failed to do so. Whatever may be the true relation between Asser and Einhard, however, the Frankish influence in the present work is apparent. It has been pointed out by Mr. Stevenson that its peculiar form may be paralleled in lives of Lewis the Pious, and it may be added that in his use of certain words Asser has adopted the Frankish signification. An example is the translation of the Anglo-Saxon "aldor mon," or "ealdorman," by "comes." So strongly marked is the Frankish element that it has even been used as an argument against the authenticity of the *Life*, but this objection may be met by a reference to the close connection between Wessex and Gaul at this period. It is to be remembered that Ethelwulf had married the daughter of Charles the Bald; that the frequent missions to Rome had necessarily to pass through the Frankish dominions; and that Alfred had imported from the Continent both scholars and monks.

Moreover, if the Frankish element in the *Life* is evident, the Welsh element is still more clear. Asser is careful to note the situation of most of the places which he mentions, as, for example, London, Reading and Sheppey. He supplies the Welsh equivalents of many place names. But while these notes can hardly have been intended for the benefit of any one except his British readers, there is even stronger evidence of the Welsh origin of the work. The use of "dextralis," right-hand, in the sense of "southern," and of "sinistralis" in the sense of "northern," would have been impossible for any one but a Welshman; and it is significant that our author does not explain the position of such Welsh places as he mentions, or give the Anglo-Saxon equivalents of their names. He shows an intimate knowledge of current events in Wales, and it must be concluded, from internal evidence, that the work was written by a Welshman for Welshmen.

A further peculiarity of Asser is his fondness for supporting his statements by an appeal to personal knowledge. He has seen the Ashdown thorn and the fortress of Cynwit; he has heard the story of Queen Eadburh from Alfred's own lips, and has listened to the king's lamentations on the difficulties with which he met in his pursuit of knowledge. Indeed, throughout the *Life*, there is a constant declaration that " quorum pars magna fui."

Finally, the present work is marked by a strong tendency to exaggeration and to idealisation. The account which is given, for example, of the life of the children of Alfred at their father's court is obviously not to be taken literally; such perfect children have never existed, and the degree of civilisation which is implied is far too high for the period. Other instances of what has been called the Celtic "rebellion against facts" will be found in the text; it is enough to say that, however much Asser may have admired his "truth-telling lord," he did not feel called upon to imitate him very closely.

The Purpose of the Life of Alfred. It may be presumed that Asser had some motive in writing a life of Alfred, but it is by no means easy to say what that motive was. On the face of it, it is a little peculiar that a Welshman should become the biographer of a West Saxon king, even though he had spent much time at that king's court. Our author himself gives us little or no help. On two occasions, indeed, he does mention the proposed contents of his work, telling us that it is his intention to record what he knows of the life and character of the king and some of his deeds. But in neither place does he say anything as to the circumstances which moved him to undertake the work. It may, however, be noted that the book is not intended as a formal biography on the author's own showing, while his statement is borne out by the fact that many of the annals contained in the book bear no direct relation to the events of Alfred's life. Nor was the book in any sense meant as a complete history of the reign, since it was written while the king was still alive. It is rather an account of a certain side of Alfred's life, and a description of a certain side of his character.

For such a work the most obvious motive would be found in the natural inclination of a man to produce a panegyric on his benefactor. Alfred had been the benefactor both of Asser and of Asser's Church, and he was in every way a suitable subject for a panegyrist's talent. But the *Life* most certainly is not a panegyric in the ordinary sense. Except in the opening passage, which may be regarded as a dedication, but also may be equally well regarded as an expression of the pious wishes of the author, Alfred is nowhere addressed. On the contrary, he is quoted as the authority for some of the author's statements. Nor, it may be supposed, would the scandal of the West Saxon royal house have been included in a formal panegyric, even though Alfred were fond of telling one of the scandalous stories. And it is surely certain that the truth-loving king would have been offended rather than pleased by the extravagant idealisation of his personal character and of his administration.

It is even fairly obvious that the book was not primarily intended for English readers. So far as Asser takes up a definite attitude with regard to Wessex, it is to regard it as a foreign country; a fact which is the more remarkable when we remember that he was spending much of his time at the court of its king. Thus he explains that Cynwit was only fortified " in our manner," where " our " clearly means British as opposed to Saxon; and he calls Wessex " that " land. Again, as has been already pointed out, he fails to explain the situation of places in Wales, or to give the Saxon equivalents of Welsh place-names, if such equivalents existed. Had the book been intended for English readers, it was surely more needful to explain the position of Glewissig or Brecheiniog to the people of Wessex than to explain that of London for the benefit of the people of Wales. It seems as if Asser hardly antici-

pated that his work would be read in England.   On the
other hand, it is abundantly clear that he did expect that
it would be read in Wales, and that it was essentially
intended for Welshmen.

If, therefore, a motive can be discovered at all, it must
be sought in Wales rather than in England, and it is
perhaps in the political situation in the former country that
we may find the reason which led Asser to supply his
countrymen with a biography of an alien king, with a
biography, moreover, of so peculiar a character.

Of that situation the most prominent characteristic was
the conflict of two policies.   In the crisis of the Danish
invasions, neutrality was an impossibility, and the princes
of Wales had to make their choice between alliance with
the invader and alliance with the English.   To make
common cause with the heathen, to avail themselves of the
opportunity for revenge, to use the difficulties of the West
Saxon and Mercian kings as a means for effecting the
consolidation and even the extension of their country, was
undoubtedly an attractive line of action.   And under the
influence of Rhodri Mawr this policy had been pursued,
and, on the whole, pursued with some success.   His
defeat and death did not result in an immediate change of
attitude on the part of his sons ; Anaraut remained in
alliance with the Northumbrian Danes.   And though
there was an eventual change, it can hardly be doubted
that the newly-formed West Saxon connection was in

need of strengthening, or that it was not universally popular.

It has been already pointed out that Asser was a politician as well as an ecclesiastic and a scholar. His residence at the court of Alfred had a quasi-political character; he was to plead the cause of his Church against King Hemeid, and perhaps to plead the cause of the whole district which suffered at Hemeid's hands. For such a man it was impossible to remain indifferent as to the general relations between his countrymen and their neighbours, and Asser soon adopted a definite line. Both his residence in Wessex and his profession may have assisted in forming his opinion; in any case he was strongly pro-Saxon. That this was his attitude appears from the way in which he is careful to add to his description of the eventual submission of Anaraut, that from his Danish alliance he "had gained no good but hurt only." It is also indicated by his insistence on the advantage which accrued to those who sought and obtained the friendship of Alfred.

Having formed his opinion, he hastened to enforce it, and it was to advocate the policy which he favoured, to secure its complete adoption and continued maintenance, and to convert his opponents, that he wrote his *Life of Alfred*. It is not meant to imply that this was an appeal to a non-existent body of democratic public opinion. It was an appeal to those who read, and more especially to the clergy, whose political influence in Wales would appear to have been consistently great. As Gildas had tried to effect a reformation of private morals by narrating the disasters of his countrymen, so Asser tried to effect a reformation of public morals, to win his countrymen from their iniquitous league with the enemies of God and Holy Church, by his biography of a West Saxon king.

An examination of the contents of the *Life* would appear to support this opinion of its object. The greatest argument in favour of a union of Welsh and English against the Dane was naturally to be found in their common Christianity, while the chief obstacles to such a league were to be found in the traditional hostility between the two peoples and in the conviction which the Welsh entertained of the barbarism of the English, a conviction which had been illustrated by their unwillingness to attempt the salvation of Anglo-Saxon souls. In order, therefore, to convert the opponents of the pro-Saxon policy it was necessary to insist on the community in religion between the two peoples and on the civilisation of Wessex.

It is just upon these very points that the *Life* does lay stress. Asser is perpetually insisting on the zeal of Alfred for religion and for learning; he draws attention to the piety of Ethelwulf and Ethelred; and he declares that the unchristian conduct of Ethelbald was reprobated by his people. He devotes much of his space to the enthusiasm for learning which marked the character of Alfred, and to a description of his civilising work. And in the annalistic portion of the *Life*, it is to the common danger which threatened Christendom at the hands of the Danes that he turns the attention of his readers. It is as though he were drawing a broad picture of the perils of the age, a picture in which Alfred stands out as the laborious and successful champion of religion and of civilisation. "Should not we Christians," he seems to ask, "share in this great work, and seek the friendship of so great a king

It is, of course, true that this view of the purpose of Asser's work is open to question and can in no sense be regarded as proved. But while no other explanation is feasible, this not merely fits the character of the book, but may even be said to account for it. It can explain the presence of details concerning the attacks of the Danes on the Frankish kingdoms, for those details, however apparently alien to a life of Alfred, might serve to show what was to be expected at the hands of the heathen, and tnat the peril from them was not yet passed. Indeed the annalistic portion of the *Life*, which seems at first sight rather out of place and somewhat purposeless, assumes a new interest if the whole work be regarded as a plea for common action against the Dane, and as an attempt to display Alfred as the hero of a threatened Christendom. And finally, it is no longer surprising that so much of our

author's attention should be directed to the literary and
religious side of the king's work. It may perhaps be
suggested that Asser as a scholar and an ecclesiastic would
naturally insist on this side, and this is no doubt true.
But the circumstances of the author's life are hardly
sufficient to account for the comparative, and in some
instances complete, neglect with which so many of
Alfred's activities are treated. On the other hand, if the
view here put forward be correct, the peculiar shape of
the work is almost ideal for the purpose for which it was
produced.

The relation of the Life of Alfred to the Chronicle.

That there is a very intimate connection
between the annalistic portion of the *Life* and the
Chronicle is apparent from the most superficial comparison of the two works. On closer investigation we
are compelled to believe that the Latin annals are, in the
main, merely a rendering of the Anglo-Saxon, with
certain additions to which allusion has already been made.
The converse view has, indeed, been put forward, and it
has been practically suggested that Asser wrote the
Chronicle, while Pauli would trace both to a common
Latin original. So far as the latter suggestion is concerned, it is, perhaps, enough to say with Mr. Stevenson
that no evidence for the existence of such an original has
ever been produced. Nor is it possible to regard the
annals contained in the *Life* as the basis of those

in the *Chronicle*.   Unless we regard his text as being
here corrupted, our author on one occasion falls into error
owing to the fact that he did not understand his original;
in describing the flight of the Danes from Wareham, the
accepted reading of Asser declares that the pagans committed the peculiarly foolish blunder of killing all their
horsemen, or at least all their horses.   Again, in certain
cases where our author supplies the Anglo-Saxon equivalents of place-names, he gives the dative plural in place of
the nominative, writing Suth-Seaxum for Suth-Seaxe,
and so forth.   As Mr. Plummer points out, this certainly
appears to prove that he was translating from an Anglo-
Saxon original, possessing only an imperfect knowledge of
the language which he was reading.   On these and similar
grounds it must be admitted that the annalistic portion of
the *Life* is based directly on the *Chronicle*.

Yet Asser must not be regarded as having followed his
authority slavishly.   Sometimes he adds to our knowledge.
It is to him that we owe the fact that Alfred accompanied
his father on the latter's journey to Rome, there being no
reason for thinking that he remained there in the interval
between his first visit and the arrival of Ethelwulf.   He
supplies us with the story of the rebellion of Ethelbald,
which is not found elsewhere, though it may possibly be
hinted at.   And in this connection he adds to the
Chronicle's account of the joy with which Ethelwulf was
greeted on his return the statement that his people were

anxious to expel his rebellious son. Other examples of
additions will be found in the notes. In one place it is at
least possible that Asser has preserved a more accurate
account of an event than that which appears in the
Chronicle, namely, in his description of the battle of
Ashdown and of the part played in it by Ethelred. In
short, while our author makes use of the Anglo-Saxon
annals, he leaves himself free to add to it and to amend it
when he has additional sources of information.

This connection between the *Life* and the *Chronicle*
has been used as the basis for an attack upon the authenticity of the former. But it would appear to be established that the Anglo-Saxon annals were actually begun
in the reign of Alfred, and if this be admitted nothing
would be more natural, as Mr. Stevenson has pointed out,
than that a Welshman should make use of an existing
narrative of events which occurred before his arrival in
Wessex. It may, perhaps, be suggested with regard to
the annals subsequent to the year 884, that here the
Chronicle and Asser drew from a common source.
These annals are mainly concerned with the affairs of the
Continent, about which neither the compilers of the
Chronicle nor our author could have any first-hand information. But, when every allowance has been made for
Asser's additions and modifications, and for the possibility
that on occasion both the *Life* and the *Chronicle* are based
on a third source, the fact remains that the annalistic

portion of the former adds very little to our knowledge, and must be considered as being to all intents and purposes a Latin version of the Anglo-Saxon, edited for the benefit of Welsh readers.

Historical Value of the Life of Alfred. In view of the comparative unimportance of the annals which are incorporated in the *Life*, it is clear that it is upon the biographical portion of the work that any estimate of the historical value of the whole must be based. But to form any such estimate is a matter of extreme difficulty. In the first place, the text of our author is marred by many interpolations, and it is by no means easy to distinguish between the genuine work of Asser and the matter which has been grafted on to it. The absence of any manuscript of the *Life of Alfred* makes all such distinction somewhat problematical; the most that can be secured is practical certainty by the route of plausible conjecture. One editor has accepted passages which another rejects, and in one case at least there is reason to question the authenticity of a passage which has been accepted by the latest editor of the text of Asser. Nor have we only to meet the difficulty of additions to the genuine work of our author; it is always possible and sometimes probable that there have been omissions. There is not wanting evidence that the manuscript was very carelessly transcribed.

A second difficulty arises from the very cause to which

the *Life* mainly owes its interest and its importance. The majority of the facts recorded by our author occur nowhere else, and we have, therefore, in most instances no means whereby we may check the accuracy of his statements.   On very rare occasions it is true that some light is indirectly thrown upon the text by .the king's own works and by the evidence of the contemporary Frankish historians, Prudentius and Hincmar.   In the former we have evidence that Asser did assist Alfred in his literary labours, for he is "thanked" in the Preface to the *Pastoral Care*.   We have too the royal declaration of his educational ideals to bear out what our author says concerning his zeal for learning.   In the Frankish writers we find some little additional authority ; Prudentius, for example, supporting the story of Ethelbald's marriage to Judith.   But for the most part we must judge Asser by himself, and we cannot test any considerable number of his original contributions by reference to other authors.

There is, however, every reason to believe that in his main facts at least our author is accurate.   Residing, as he did, for a large part of his time at the court of Alfred and enjoying daily intercourse with the king, he was obviously in a position to describe that king's character and labours.   Unless, therefore, we believe either that he was incapable of understanding aright that which he saw or that he was a deliberate liar, we must admit his substantial accuracy.   And there is no reason for thinking that he was either a fool or worse. We may not have a very high opinion of his intellectual attainments, but we must surely allow that he was possessed of ordinary intelligence, and if this be so, he can hardly have failed altogether to understand the conditions in which he passed much of his time. That he should have lied deliberately is still more out of the question. He was writing on a subject concerning which gross inaccuracy would have been patent even to his Welsh readers. In the second place, whatever may be the precise value of Asser's work, we must surely think that Alfred was an honest man who would have reprobated deliberate misstatements. And this being the case, our author, from self-interest, if from no higher cause, would have avoided giving offence to his patron. It may be suggested, moreover, that if the view of the purpose of the work already set forth be just, that work would have defeated its own end if it had consisted of a collection of baseless legends. The balance of probability would, then, seem to be in favour of regarding the account which Asser gives of the king and his court as substantially truthful.

At the same time there is every reason to regard that account as idealised and exaggerated. We cannot accept as literally true the author's description of the royal household, which is false alike to the period and to human nature. Nor can it be doubted that there is gross exaggeration in the account of the administration of the

king.   Upon the brighter side of that picture little more
reliance can be placed than upon the later mediæval story
that in Alfred's time a man might leave a purse full of
gold by the wayside and find it untouched after many days.

Our conclusion, then, must be that the *Life* is not to
be taken too literally, that it should be subjected to judi-
cious criticism.   Alfred was not all that he is represented
to be by our author, nor was his reign a golden age.
The best of kings cannot wholly free their country from
distress and from vice, and we may be sure that theft and
injustice, poverty and crime, continued even while Alfred
ruled.   Yet when this has been said, when we have
admitted the necessity for rejecting the pseudo-Asser and
for toning down the genuine, the *Life* still remains a
work of the very highest importance.   It supplies us with
most of the details that we possess concerning the king,
and since in the course of history we so rarely meet with
a character which is not merely great but also truly good,
the details which bring such a character home to us can
never be regarded as trivial additions to our knowledge
of the past.

Asser's Character of Alfred.   So much has
been written concerning the character of Alfred the
Great that some apology is needed for dealing with a
subject which has been already dealt with so fully.   But
it may not be out of place to attempt to show what
manner of man he is represented as being in the pages of

Asser. And in the first place it is worth while to notice that in the *Life* we have two distinct and even conflicting portraits of the king. The first represents him as he appeared to our author, the second as he appeared to the somewhat distorted vision of mediæval monasticism. It is with the former of these two portraits that we would deal at present.

In the genuine Asser, then, Alfred stands out first of all as the strong man struggling with adversity and gaining a hard-won triumph. He is beset with dangers and trials, and has but few human helpers. Those for whom he toils are careless and almost hostile, while he is the victim of physical weakness which makes life still harder. But he does not despair even in the darkest hour, for he believes in the justice of his cause and is supported by the conviction that, come what may, he must still do his duty. Above all, he puts his trust in God, crying with the Psalmist, " I will yet give him thanks, which is the help of my countenance, and my God." It is this living faith in a Higher Power which makes it possible for him to persevere; he is deeply and sincerely religious. But he is no pietist. His religion is practical; he will not neglect the duty of governing and saving his country in order to visit the tombs of the Apostles, nor will he risk the safety of his army for the sake of performing his private devotions. " Whatsoever thy hand findeth to do, do it with thy might," would serve as his motto. He

believes in the active life : he is an accomplished hunter
and excels in manly sports, despite his ill-health ; he
lives laborious days.

On the other hand, while he is no bookworm, he is
fully alive to the importance of training the mind no less
than the body ; he is profoundly convinced of the value
of education both for the ruler and the ruled.   Every
minute that he can spare is devoted to the improvement
of his mind, and when the danger from foreign attack
has for a while passed away, his first care is to make good
the moral damage, which that attack has caused, by the
promotion of civilisation.   Here again he long sought
help and opportunity in vain.   His intense desire for
learning had been thwarted in his early youth, and as he
grew to manhood the peril of the state deprived him of
the needed leisure.   Even when opportunity was at last
granted to him, he had not merely to contend with past
neglect but also to create the means which should make
intellectual advance a possibility.   But he does this and
more.   His naturally quick intelligence was displayed in
all his work, and it enabled him to make good the deficiencies in his education.   His indomitable will helped
him to overcome all other obstacles, permitting neither
the lack of early training, nor the many other cares of
his position, nor the slackness of his subjects, to
deter him from the successful pursuit of his object.   He
educated himself and his people, almost forcing the

latter to learn for their own good, despite their great reluctance.

It is recorded by Asser that Alfred kept ever by him a little book, which contained, amongst other things, certain favourite psalms. It is hardly an extravagant assumption that among those psalms was the eighty-second; that he was familiar with the Psalmist's injunctions to the judges, "Defend the poor and fatherless: see that such as are in need and necessity have right." Such at least was the king's constant endeavour. To those who had no helper, he was a zealous friend, careful to inquire into the decisions of the judges and to correct wrong judgments. Yet he was patient and gentle in correction; only when persuasion and advice had failed to bring about the needed reformation did he resort to actual upbraiding. No doubt his own supreme integrity lent additional weight to his admonitions; in any case, the moral force of the king was so great that erring judges were as much affected by his mild rebukes as they would have been by the severest punishment, if inflicted by another man.

In his private, no less than in his public character, Alfred excelled. At a time when morality was low, he was conspicuous in this regard. He tried to realise his high ideals of a father's duty by the careful training of his children, giving to them all that he had been himself denied. He was devoted to the truth above all things;

he was generous to all who came to him, a friend to strangers, hospitable. None, we are told, failed to win from him just consideration; his good-will was a real benefit to all who secured it.

Such is Alfred as his Welsh friend and biographer draws him for us. It is the portrait of a great man and of a great king, but it is much more. It is the portrait of a good man also. For a Napoleon we may feel admiration: our admiration cannot be withheld from Alfred, but it may well be kindled into love.

The Interpolations in the Life of Alfred. That the *Life of Alfred*, as we possess it, has been much interpolated is quite obvious from the internal evidence of the text. Various passages bear on their surface all the marks of being later additions. We have the cowherd's wife, in the story of the cakes, rebuking the king in verse, while on another occasion the author is made to refer his readers to the Annals of Saint Neot, a compilation which was not produced until a century or two after his death. So much is clearly established, but when we come to the less obvious additions, we are at once met with difficulties. In the absence of any MS. of the *Life*, we are forced to rely mainly on the authority of the only edition produced with reference to the lost MS. and also marking the additions to it; on the evidence of the existing later transcripts; and on the chroniclers who made use of Asser in their compilations. Of these last, by far the most important is Florence of Worcester, who possessed considerable critical faculty and who has made much use of the *Life*. From him it is possible to arrive at the true reading on occasion, and from him one passage, the account of the battle of Mertun, has perhaps been recovered. So valuable is he, that the latest editor of the work has relied very largely upon him in the task of reconstructing Asser's text, and has on at least one very important occasion thought it right to modify the account of an event by an addition derived only from Florence. Help is also given by Simeon of Durham, though to nothing like the same extent. But, even with such assistance, it is clear that in many instances the emendation of the text must depend solely on conjecture.

It is to the misplaced energy of Archbishop Parker, the original editor of Asser, that most of the interpolations are to be attributed. They are of two descriptions. On the one hand we have additions both of single words and phrases, and of longer passages, which are derived from the Annals of Saint Neot, which were wrongly attributed to our author. On the other hand, Parker and Camden have interpolated matter from other writers and from their own imagination.

Among the interpolations from the Annals, the story of the burning of the cakes is far and away the most important, since it has become inseparably connected with the name of Alfred in the popular imagination. Another important addition is that which immediately follows, the representation of the king as a reformed tyrant. In the text, and in the notes on the interpolated passages, the other additions will be found. It may be mentioned that occasionally the interpolations supply a correction, as, for instance, the mention of the sack of London in 851.

There is one interpolation which compels us, however reluctantly, to regard the eminent antiquary Camden as a somewhat inexpert forger. Carried away by his desire to support the claims of Oxford in the futile dispute with Cambridge concerning priority of foundation, he forgot to be honest and attempted to place the case of his own University in an unassailable position. For this purpose Asser was utilised. As Alfred was the creator of shires and hundreds, the navy and the law, there could be no better way of proving the antiquity of Oxford than by showing that the very man who founded all the other institutions of this country could only reform the University. We find, therefore, an attempt on the part of Grimbald to dictate to the ninth century Hebdomadal Council, which retorts that Gildas and Nennius, Melkin and Kentigern, had approved of its constitution, while Saint Germanus, after crushing the Pelagian heresy, had apparently received the fifth century equivalent of the modern honorary degree. Grimbald is unconvinced, and a royal commission is appointed to inquire into the state of the University, with the result that the saint removes himself (and his coffin) to Winchester, defeated and disgusted. If this does not seem to be a very serious treatment of the interpolation, it may be pointed out that it is itself the merest nonsense, and that the only remarkable thing about it is that the story should have been accepted at all, even in the seventeenth century and by bitter controversialists.

At the close of the *Life*, we have three Parkerian interpolations. One from the Annals relates the death of Alfred; one from Henry of Huntingdon contains that writer's metrical panegyric on the king; and one from Bale is a little note about the death of Asser.

There remains one further passage which has met with general acceptance and which yet appears to bear all the distinctive marks of an interpolation. After an account of the illness which attacked Alfred in the midst of his wedding festivities, the text of the *Life* proceeds to a rambling description of previous physical afflictions from which the king had suffered. In the story as we have it there are inconsistencies and difficulties past solution, while Alfred appears in it as morbidly religious and rather weak. On these and other grounds, which are set forth in full in the notes, it is hardly possible to accept the passage as being the work of Asser, and the conclusion must be that it originated in the two facts that Alfred never enjoyed really robust health and that at the time of his wedding he was seized with sudden and severe illness. The rest of the passage would seem to be a late elaboration, while the apparent reference to it in later portions of the *Life* may be regarded either as modification of the genuine text to suit the interpolation, or rather perhaps as the result of the author's natural tendency to hyperbole.

In conclusion, it must be added that there is always a possibility that passages which are universally regarded as being the work of Asser are not so in actual fact. We can never be sure that the whole corruption of the text has been fathomed.

Alfred as he appears in the Interpolations. It is in the interpolations that we find that second portrait of Alfred to which allusion has been already made. It is a portrait which bears the same relation to that contained in the genuine text as an inferior copy of an old master does to its original. In place of the strong man, we have a weakling or a tyrant. At the beginning of his reign he was guilty of flagrant misrule, and it was only the troubles which deservedly fell upon him and the stern rebukes of Saint Neot that weaned him from his evil courses. Yet, and the inconsistency may be noted, he was ever a pietist, one who from his earliest childhood resorted to the shrines of saints. He refuses to battle with temptation, and prays that he may be so afflicted with physical illness that the exercise of self-control may be no longer needful. Much of his time is spent in association with his shadowy, though saintly, "relative" Neot; and he relies mainly on miraculous interventions of Heaven to enable him to overcome his difficulties. In the crisis of his fate, when the very existence of his kingdom is in danger, he does not devote himself to the task of nerving his subjects to one last effort. On the contrary he withdraws to the wastes of Somerset and wanders from hovel to hovel. In place of organising victory, he proves himself to be a somewhat incompetent cook.

All this is as unlike the genuine Alfred as it could possibly be. For strength we have weakness; for steady devotion to duty, selfishness or despair; for stern resistance to temptation, a cowardly seeking for a way of escape. His generosity and kindliness are turned to coldness and pride; his love of justice to love of pleasure. And if he does reform, it is only from fear of punishment. In a word, he is no longer Alfred the Great: he has deteriorated into a pale replica of a third-rate mediæval saint. If there were nothing else to mark these passages as interpolations, the character of the king as depicted in them would do so. Such an ineffective pietist could never have done the work which Alfred actually accomplished. He would have imitated Burhred of Mercia, and sought peace at the tombs of the Apostles.

Editions and Translations of Asser. During the Middle Ages the *Life* was freely used by three chroniclers. Florence of Worcester, who died about

1118, practically incorporated it in his *Chronicon ex Chronicis*, though he revised Asser's Latin and rearranged his materials. Reference has already been made to the value of Florence as a guide to the genuine text of the *Life*. Simeon of Durham, under Henry I, and the Cuthbertine monk whose annals were used by Simeon, both made use of Asser, the former keeping much more closely to the original. William of Malmesbury, who died in 1143, adopts much of the work in his *Gesta Regum Anglorum*, though mainly in an abbreviated form and with considerable modifications.

The *Life of Alfred* was first printed by Archbishop Parker in 1574, from a manuscript which was entirely destroyed in the fire in the Cottonian Library in 1731. As has been mentioned, the Archbishop added much to the original. In 1603, Camden reprinted Parker's edition with the addition of the Oxford interpolation, in his *Anglica, Normannica, Hibernica, Cambrica a veteribus scripta*, published at Frankfort. Wise, in 1722, published a third edition, in which an attempt was made to distinguish between the genuine text and the interpolations by means of a reference to the MS. But he did not undertake the collation personally, and Hill, to whom the work was entrusted, was careless. In 1848 a further edition appeared in the *Monumenta Historica Britannica*, under the editorship of Petrie, in which the interpolations were more clearly marked by being placed within square brackets.

Even this method, however, did not prove entirely successful. Finally, in 1904, Mr. W. H. Stevenson published the text, with valuable corrections, distinguishing between the genuine matter and the false by means of differences in type.

Various translations have appeared. Dr. Giles included it in his *Six Old English Chroniclers*, in Bohn's Antiquarian Library, 1848. It is translated by the Rev. J. Stevenson, in the second volume of his *Church Historians of England*, 1854; by Mr. Conybeare in his *Alfred in the Chroniclers*, 1900; and by Professor Albert S. Cook, of Yale, 1906, who had the advantage of the use of Mr. Stevenson's text and notes.

The Present Translation. The present translation has been prepared from the text in the *Monumenta Historica Britannica*, though regard has been paid to the emendations of that text which have been suggested since its publication. The interpolated passages have, it is hoped, been clearly marked off from the genuine text by being placed in italics, and the same system has been adopted in the notes, those on the interpolated passages being given in a distinct section. An attempt has been made to enable the reader easily to discover what is the genuine work of Asser, and what additional matter supplied by his editors.

L. Cecil Jane

TABLE OF CONTENTS

DOMINO MEO VENERABILI PIISSIMOQUE·
OMNIVM BRITTANNIE INSVLAE xpiANO
RVM RECTORI· ælfRED· ANGLORVM SAXO
NVM REGI· ASSER· OMNIVM· SERVO
RVM DEI VLTIMVS· MILLE MODAM
ADVOTA DESIDERIORVM· VTRIVSQVE
VITAE PROSPERITATEM·

ANNO DOMINICAE
INCARNATIONIS· DCCC·XLIX· natus
est ælfred angul saxonum rex in uilla
regia que dicitur nuanating· in uilla p̄aga
que nominat̄ berrocscire que pagata hr̄ er
uocatur aberrocsilua ubibuxus babundan
eissime naseit̄ cuius genelogia tali serie

Specimen of the lost manuscript, reproduced from the edition
of F. Wise, 1722.

ASSER'S LIFE OF ALFRED

THE AUTHOR'S PRAYER.

To my honoured and most pious lord, to the ruler of all the Christians of the Island of Britain, to Alfred, of the Angles and Saxons king, Asser, the least of all the servants of God, wishes all manner of prosperity in this life and in that which is to come, according to the prayers of his fervent desires.

CONCERNING THE BIRTH AND GENEALOGY OF ALFRED.

A.D. 849.   In the year of the Incarnation of the Lord eight hundred and forty-nine, Alfred, king of the Anglo-Saxons, was born at the royal residence which is called Wantage, in the district named Berkshire.   And that district is so named from the wood of Berroc, where grows the box-tree in great plenty.

Now his genealogy is traced in the following manner : King Alfred was the son of King Ethelwulf, which was the son of Egbert, which was the son of Ealhmund, which was the son of Eafa, which was the son of Eoppa, which was the son of Ingild.   Ingild and Ine, the famous

king of the West Saxons, were brothers of the full blood ;
and this Ine went to Rome, and there, ending this present
life with honour, departed to the heavenly country to reign
with Christ.   They were the sons of Cenred, which was the
son of Ceowald, which was the son of Cuda, which
was the son of Cuthwin, which was the son of Ceawlin,
which was the son of Cynric, which was the son of
Creoda, which was the son of Cerdic, which was the son
of Elesa, which was the son of Gewis, from whom the
Britons call all that people Gegwis.   He was the son of
Brond, which was the son of Belde, which was the son of
Woden, which was the son of Frithowald, which was the
son of Frealaf, which was the son of Frithuwulf, which
was the son of Fingodwulf, which was the son of Geata.

This Geta the heathen long since worshipped as a god,
and of him the poet Sedulius, in his Paschal Hymn,
makes mention, saying, "With solemn measures, and
tragic cries, or the absurd Geta, or with what form you
will of the poetic art, heathen poets labour to adorn
their idle tales, bringing back the taint of deadly sin into
our lives, and, slaves to custom, writing many a lying
book.   Why, then, should I keep silence concerning
the great and marvellous deeds of Christ the Saviour ?   I,
who ofttimes chant praises in songs of David, upon an
instrument of ten strings, and make heavenly psalmody
with no pomp of words ! "

This Geata was the son of Caetwa, which was the son

of Beaw, which was the son of Sceldwaea, which was the
son of Heremod, which was the son of Itermod, which
was the son of Hathra, which was the son of Huala,
which was the son of Bedwig, which was the son of
Sem, which was the son of Noe, which was the son of
Lamech, which was the son of Methusalem, which was
the son of Enoch, which was the son of Jared, which
was the son of Malaleel, which was the son of Cainan,
which was the son of Enos, which was the son of Seth,
which was the son of Adam.

Concerning the Genealogy of his Mother.

Now his mother was called Osburh, a woman deeply
religious, noble in character, and noble also by descent.
She was the daughter of Oslac, the renowned butler of
King Ethelwulf. This Oslac was a Goth by race, for he
was descended from Goths and Jutes, being of the seed of
Stuf and Wihtgar, two brothers, and also ealdormen, who
received authority over the Isle of Wight from their uncle,
King Cerdic, and from his son Cynric, their cousin. And
they slew the few British inhabitants of the island, as
many as they found therein, at a place which is called
Wihtgaraburh : for the rest of the natives of that island
had either been killed already or had fled into exile.

How the Men of Devon Beat the Pagans, and how the Pagans Wintered in Sheppey.

A.D. 851. In the year of the Incarnation of the Lord eight hundred and fifty-one, which was the third year from the birth of King Alfred, Ceorl, ealdorman of Devon, with the men of Devon, fought against the heathen in a place that is called Wicganbeorg, and the Christians had the victory.

In that same year the heathen for the first time wintered in the island that is called Sheppey, which being interpreted is the isle of sheep. It lies in the river Thames, between the East Saxons and the men of Kent, but is nearer to Kent than to the East Saxons. And in it a most excellent monastery has been built.

How the Pagans Beat the King of the Mercians.

Moreover, in this year the army of the heathen came into the mouth of the river Thames with three hundred and fifty ships. They laid waste Dorubernia, that is the city of the men of Kent, and the city of London, which stands on the northern bank of the river Thames, on the border of the East Saxons and the Middle Saxons, but yet that city in truth belongs to the East Saxons. Then they put to flight Beortulf, king of the Mercians, and all his host, who had come out to battle against them.

How the Pagans were Beaten by King Ethelwulf.

When such things had there come to pass, the army of the pagans went into Surrey, which is a district on the southern bank of the river Thames, to the westward of Kent. And Ethelwulf, king of the West Saxons, and Ethelbald, his son, with the whole army, fought for a very long while in the place that is called Aclea, which is, the oak in the mead. There, when both armies had fought boldly and fiercely for a long while, the greater part of the pagan host was utterly destroyed and slain, so that never in any land have we heard of such slaughter of them in one day, either before or since. And the Christians gained a glorious victory and held the field of blood.

How King Athelstan Beat the Pagans.

In the selfsame year did Athelstan the king, and Ealhere the ealdorman, overthrow a great army of pagans in Kent, at a place called Sandwich, and took from them nine ships. The rest escaped by flight.

How King Ethelwulf came to the Help of the King of the Mercians.

A.D. 853. In the year of the Incarnation of the Lord eight hundred and fifty-three, which was the

eleventh year from the birth of King Alfred, Burhred,
king of the Mercians, sent messengers to Ethelwulf, king
of the West Saxons.   And he prayed him to send him
help that he might bring under his authority the Mid-
Britons, who dwell between Mercia and the western sea,
and who greatly rebelled against him.   And when he
had received this message, King Ethelwulf without delay
advanced with his army and went into the land of the
Britons with King Burhred.   Forthwith, entering that land,
he wasted it and brought it under the authority of King
Burhred, and when he had so done he returned home.

How Alfred went First to Rome.

In the same year King Ethelwulf sent the same Alfred,
his son, to Rome in the company of many both gentle
and simple.   The Lord Pope Leo then held the apostolic see.   He received the said child Alfred, and fully
anointed him as king and confirmed him, making him
his own son by adoption.

How the Saxons Fought the Pagans in Thanet, and how the Daughter of King Ethelwulf was Wedded.

In this year also Ealhere the ealdorman, with the men
of Kent, and Huda, with the men of Surrey, fought
bravely and boldly with the army of the heathen in the

island which in the Saxon tongue is called Thanet, but in
the British Ruim. And at first the Christians had the
victory. And when the battle was long continued in that
place, very many fell on both sides and were swallowed
up in the water and so drowned ; and both those ealdormen fell there.

It was in this year also that Ethelwulf, king of the
West Saxons, after Eastertide, gave his daughter to
Burhred, king of the Mercians, to be his queen. And
the marriage was celebrated with royal pomp in the king's
residence which is called Chippenham

How the Pagans Wintered in Sheppey the Second
    Time, and Concerning Edmund, King of the
    East Angles.

A.D. 855. In the year of the Incarnation of the Lord
eight hundred and fifty-five, which was the seventh year
from the birth of the said king, *Edmund, the most glorious
king of the East Angles, began to reign on the eighth day
before the calends of January, that is on the day of the
Nativity of the Lord, being in the fourteenth year of his age.
And in this year also died Lothar, Roman emperor, son of
Lewis, the most pious Angustus. And in this year, which
was the first of the Emperor Charles III, son of Lewis II,*
a great army of pagans passed the whole winter in the
same island of Sheppey.

How King Ethelwulf gave Gifts to God, and how Alfred went to Rome the Second Time.

In the same year did the said revered King Ethelwulf deliver the tenth part of his whole realm from all service to the king and from taxation, and by a perpetual grant sacrificed it on the cross of Christ to the One and Triune God, for the salvation of his soul and for the salvation of the souls of his ancestors.

And in the same year he went to Rome with great honour, and he took his said son Alfred with him on that journey for the second time. For he loved him above his other sons. And there he remained one full year, and when it had passed, he returned to his own land, bringing with him Judith, daughter of Charles, king of the Franks.

How Ethelbald, the King's Son, Conspired against the King.

But while King Ethelwulf was abiding across the sea for some small space of time, an evil thing, and one which was contrary to all Christian feeling, arose in the western part of Selwood. For King Ethelbald, and Ealhstan, bishop of the church of Sherborne, and Eanwulf, ealdorman of the district of Somerset, are said to have conspired to prevent King Ethelwulf, when he returned again from

Rome, from being ever received in the kingdom. Now very many ascribe this evil deed, unparalleled in all ages, to the bishop and to the ealdorman alone, to whose advice the origin of the deed is traced. But there are also many who attribute it solely to royal pride, because that king was also froward in this and many other wrongful acts. So have we heard from the accounts of certain men, and the outcome of the event agrees with this opinion.

How King Ethelwulf Returned from Rome and how He showed Wondrous Clemency.

For when King Ethelwulf was now returning from Rome, his same son and all his counsellors, or rather those lying in ambush with him, tried to commit the great crime of preventing the king from entering his own realm. But neither would God permit this to come to pass, nor would the nobles of all the Saxon land agree thereto. For lest, while father and son contended, or rather while the whole people were in rebellion against both, the irreparable danger arising for the Saxon land from the civil war might grow day by day more bitter and more cruel, by the wonderful mercy of the father, and with the assent of all the nobles, the kingdom, which had before been united, was divided between father and son. And the eastern districts were assigned to the father and the

western to the son, but wrongly so. For where the
father should in justice have ruled, there reigned that
wicked and froward son, since the western portion of the
Saxon land has ever been of greater account than the
eastern.

Therefore when King Ethelwulf returned from Rome,
all that people as was right so rejoiced at the coming of
the old man, that, had he allowed it, they would have
altogether expelled his froward son Ethelbald from the
kingdom. But he, as we have said, with great forbear-
ance, and following wise counsel, would not so have it,
lest danger might result for the realm.

How King Ethelwulf caused Judith, his Wife, to Share His Throne.

And without any dispute with his nobles, and without
rousing their anger, he commanded Judith, the daughter
of King Charles, whom he had received from her father,
to sit beside him on his throne, to the end of his days,
contrary to the wrong custom of that people. For the
race of the West Saxons does not allow a queen to sit
beside a king, or even permit her to bear the title of
queen, but she is called the king's wife. This objection,
or rather this evil thing, is declared by the old men of
that people to have originated from a certain froward and
evil-minded queen of that same people. For she so acted

in every way to the hurt of her lord and all the people,
that not only did she win so much hatred towards herself
that she was driven from her queenly station, but she also
handed down the same evil to all those queens who came
after her.   For owing to the great wickedness of that
queen, all the dwellers in that land swore that no king
should be allowed to reign over them who would
command that his queen should sit beside him on a royal
throne.

The Story of Queen Eadburh.

And because, as I think, many are not aware for what
cause this wrong and hateful custom, which is contrary
to universal custom, that is, among Teutonic nations, first
arose in the Saxon land, it seems to me to be well that I
should explain the matter rather more fully.   And I have
heard this story from my truth-telling lord, Alfred, king
of the Anglo-Saxons, who has often told it to me.   He
also heard it from many sure witnesses, no small number of
whom indeed remembered the event.

There was not long since in Mercia a certain able king,
Offa by name, who was feared by all the kings, his
neighbours, and by all the nations round about: who also
commanded a great dyke to be made from sea to sea
between the land of the Britons and Mercia.   Now
Beorhtric, king of the West Saxons, received in marriage

the same king's daughter, who was called Eadburh. And when she had presently won the love of the king and authority over almost the whole kingdom, she began to live the life of a tyrant, after the manner of her father. She attacked any man who bore love to Beorhtric, and did all things hateful to God and men. All whom she could she accused before the king, and so by her plotting deprived them either of life or of power ; and if she could not gain their destruction from the king, she slew them with poison. It is well known that she so acted towards a certain young man, who was very dear to the king, and when she could find nothing wherewith to accuse him to the king, she killed him with poison. And of that poison the same king Beorhtric is said to have partaken unwittingly, for she desired not to give the poison to the king, but to the young man. The king, however, partook of it first and so they both perished.

Therefore when King Beorhtric was dead, as she could no longer dwell among the Saxons, she went across the sea, with vast treasures, and made her way to Charles, king of the Franks. And when she stood before the throne and proffered many gifts to the king, Charles said to her, " Choose, Eadburh, which you will have ; me or my son, who stands with me on this throne." But she made answer without thought and foolishly, and spake, saying, " If the choice is to be mine, I choose your son, since he is younger than you." Then Charles answered her, mocking her and saying, "Had you made choice of me, you should have had my son: but as you have chosen my son, you shall have neither me nor him."

Yet did he give her a great monastery of nuns, where she put off the garb of this world and put on that of the nuns. And for a very few years she held the post of abbess. But as she is said to have lived without restraint in her own land, so she was found to live with even less restraint among an alien people. For she had criminal intercourse with a certain man of her own nation, and was at last publicly convicted, and was expelled from the convent by command of King Charles, and passed her life in shame and in poverty and misery to the day of her death. So, at the last, in the company of a single slave boy, as we have heard from many eye-witnesses, she begged her bread from day to day and died wretchedly at Pavia.

CONCERNING THE WILL OF KING ETHELWULF.

So King Ethelwulf lived two years after that he was returned from Rome. And in this time he did many other things which were good for this present life, and moreover, considering that he was to pass on the way of all flesh, and that his sons after their father's death might not wrongfully contend one against the other, he gave command that a will, which was rather a letter of advice, should be written. And in it he ordered that his realm should be divided between his sons, that is, between the two eldest, and his personal inheritance between his sons and his daughter and also his relations; and in his letters did command that the money which he left behind him should be justly apportioned for the good of his soul, and to his sons, and to his nobles.

Now we have decided to record a few things out or many concerning this display of prudent foresight, that they may be observed by them that shall come after. These things are those which are known to be nearly related to the well-being of the soul. For as to the other matters, which touch the affairs of this life, there is no need to include them in this small work, lest its length should cause weariness both to those who read and to those who would fain hear it.

From the very flower of his youth he had been very zealous for the good of his soul, and for that he now commanded that his successors, after his time to the day of final judgment, should ever nourish throughout his hereditary dominions one poor man in every ten, whether born in the land or strangers, with food and drink and raiment, as long as the land should be inhabited by men and herds, and not become a desert.

Moreover he commanded that every year great store of money should be brought to Rome for the good of his soul, namely, three hundred mancuses. This he divided as follows : one hundred mancuses in honour of Saint

Peter, especially for the purchase of oil to fill all the lamps in that apostolic church on the eve of Easter and also at cockcrow: and one hundred mancuses in honour of Saint Paul, for the supply of oil in the same manner in the church of Saint Paul the Apostle, for filling the lamps on the eve of Easter and at cockcrow: and one hundred mancuses to the Catholic and apostolic pope.

How Ethelbald Ruled the West Saxons.

A.D. 858. Therefore when King Ethelwulf was dead, his son Ethelbald defied the prohibition of God, and the right custom of Christians, no less than the practice of all pagan races, and went up into his father's bed and married Judith, the daughter of Charles, king of the Franks, winning great reproach from all who heard it. Then for the space of two years and a half after his father's death he raged and ruled over the kingdom of the West Saxons.

How Edmund was Made King of the East Angles.

A.D. 856. *In the year of the Incarnation of the Lord eight hundred and fifty-six, which was the eighth year from the birth of Alfred, that is, in the second year of the Emperor Charles III, and in the eighteenth year of Ethelwulf, king of the West Saxons, Humbert, bishop of the East Angles, amid much joy and with much honour, in the royal town that*

*is called Bures, where the royal seat then was, anointed
with oil, and consecrated to be king, the most glorious
Edmund, who was then in the fourteenth year of his age,
on the sixth day of the week and on the twenty-fourth of the
month, the day of the Nativity of the Lord.*

How Ethelbert Reigned over the West Saxons.

A.D. 860.   In the year of the Incarnation of the Lord
eight hundred and sixty, which was the twelfth year from
the birth of King Alfred, Ethelbald died and was buried
at Sherborne.   Then, as was just, Ethelbert, his brother,
added Kent and Surrey and Sussex to his dominions.

In his days a great army of the heathen came by sea
and attacked the city of Winchester and sacked it.   And
as the host was returning to its ships, with great booty,
Osric, ealdorman of Hampshire, with his men, and
Ethelwulf the ealdorman, with the men of Berkshire,
manfully withstood them.   And when battle was joined
with zeal, the pagans were utterly routed, and being no
longer able to resist, they fled like women, and the
Christians held the place of slaughter.

A.D. 866.   Five years, then, reigned Ethelbert in
peace and loving-kindness, and so went the way of all
flesh, to the great sorrowing of his people.   And he rests
in peace at Sherborne, being honourably interred beside
his brother.

How the Pagans Ravaged Eastern Kent.

A.D. 864.   In the year of the Incarnation of the Lord
eight hundred and sixty-four, the pagans wintered in the
island of Thanet, and they made a sure treaty with the
men of Kent, and to them the men of Kent promised to
give money for the keeping of the treaty.   But meanwhile
the pagans, like foxes, secretly broke from their camp by
night.   For they despised the promise of money, know-
ing that they would gain more wealth from the booty
which they would steal than from peace.   So they
wasted the whole eastern portion of Kent.

How Ethelred Became King of the West Saxons.

A.D. 866.   In the year of the Incarnation of the Lord
eight hundred and sixty-six, which was the eighteenth
year from the birth of King Alfred, Ethelred, brother
of Ethelbert, king of the West Saxons, began to reign.
In the same year, a great fleet of the pagans came to Britain
from Danubia, and passed the winter in the kingdom of
the East Saxons, which in the Saxon tongue is called
East Anglia.   There they procured horses for the greater
part of the army.

Concerning the Childhood of Alfred.

But, to use nautical similies, we will no longer entrust
our ship to the waves and winds, nor will we put out far

from land and steer amid so many bloody wars and chronicles of years. For I think it well that we should return to that which chiefly led me to undertake this work, or in other words, I propose here to relate shortly what little has come to my knowledge concerning the character of my revered Lord Alfred, king of the Anglo-Saxons, in his infancy and in his boyhood.

Now he was greatly cherished above all his brothers by the united and ardent love of his father and mother, and indeed of all people ; and he was ever brought up entirely at the royal court. As he passed through his infancy and boyhood he surpassed all his brothers in beauty, and was more pleasing in his appearance, in his speech, and in his manners. From his earliest childhood the noble character of his mind gave him a desire for all things useful in this present life, and, above all, a longing for wisdom ; but, alas ! the culpable negligence of his relations, and of those who had care of him, allowed him to remain ignorant of letters until his twelfth year, or even to a later age. Albeit, day and night did he listen attentively to the Saxon poems, which he often heard others repeating, and his retentive mind enabled him to remember them.

An ardent hunter, he toiled persistently at every form of that art, and not in vain. For in his skill and success at this pursuit he surpassed all, as in all other gifts of God. And this skill we have ourselves seen on many occasions.

How Alfred Obtained a Book from his Mother, and how he was Filled with Desire of Reading.

Now it chanced on a certain day that his mother showed to him and to his brothers a book of Saxon poetry, which she had in her hand, and said, "I will give this book to that one among you who shall the most quickly learn it." Then, moved at these words, or rather by the inspiration of God, and being carried away by the beauty of the initial letter in that book, anticipating his brothers who surpassed him in years but not in grace, he answered his mother, and said, "Will you of a truth give that book to one of us? To him who shall soonest understand it and repeat it to you?" And at this she smiled and was pleased, and affirmed it, saying, "I will give it to him." Then forthwith he took the book from her hand and went to his master, and read it; and when he had read it he brought it back to his mother and repeated it to her.

After this he learnt the Daily Course, that is, the services for each hour, and then some psalms and many prayers. These were collected in one book, which, as we have ourselves seen, he constantly carried about with him everywhere in the fold of his cloak, for the sake of prayer amid all the passing events of this present life. But, alas! the art of reading which he most earnestly desired he did not acquire in accordance with his wish, because, as he was wont himself to say, in those days there were no men really skilled in reading in the whole realm of the West Saxons.

With many complaints, and with heartfelt regrets, he used to declare that among all the difficulties and trials of this life this was the greatest. For at the time when he was of an age to learn, and had leisure and ability for it, he had no masters; but when he was older, and indeed to a certain extent had anxious masters and writers, he could not read. For he was occupied day and night without ceasing both with illnesses unknown to all the physicians of that island, and with the cares of the royal office both at home and abroad, and with the assaults of the heathen by land and sea. None the less, amid the difficulties of this life, from his infancy to the present day, he has not in the past faltered in his earnest pursuit of knowledge, nor does he even now cease to long for it, nor, as I think, will he ever do so until the end of his life.

How the Pagans Attacked Northumbria.

A.D. 867. In the year of the Incarnation of the Lord eight hundred and sixty-seven, which was the nineteenth year from the birth of the said King Alfred, the same pagan army passed from the land of the East Angles to the city of York, which lies on the northern side of the river Humber.

At that time, through the promptings of the devil, very great strife had arisen among the Northumbrians, as ever happens to a people which has aroused the wrath of God. For in those days, as we have said, the Northumbrians drove out of his kingdom their rightful king, Osbert by name, and placed upon the throne a certain tyrant, called Ella, who was not of royal stock. But when the heathen came, by the inspiration of heaven, and through the efforts of the nobles for the common good, that conflict was somewhat abated, and Osbert and Ella, joining their forces and gathering an army, went to the city of York.

And, at their coming, the pagans forthwith took to flight, and tried to defend themselves within the walls of the city. Then the Christians, seeing their flight and terror, resolved to attack them even behind the defences of the city and to break down the wall. This also they did, since in those days the city had not as yet strong and enduring walls; and when the Christians had, as they planned, broken down the wall many of them also entered the city at the same time as the heathen. Then, driven by grief and despair, the heathen fell upon them fiercely, slew them, drove them in flight, and overcame them within and without the city. There were destroyed almost all the Northumbrians, and the two kings with them. And the remnant that escaped made peace with the pagans.

In this same year Ealhstan, bishop of the church of Sherborne, went the way of all flesh, after that he had ruled the see with honour for forty years ; and he was buried in peace at Sherborne.

How Alfred Married.

A.D. 868. In the year of the Incarnation of the Lord eight hundred and sixty-eight, which was the twentieth year from the birth of King Alfred, the same revered King Alfred, being then the recognised heir to the kingdom, sought and obtained a wife from Mercia. She was of noble birth, being the daughter of the ealdorman of the Gaini, Ethelred, surnamed Mucill. Her mother's name was Eadburh, of the royal stock of the king of the Mercians, and on her we often fixed the very gaze of our own eyes not many years before her death. She was a venerable matron, and for many years, from the death of her husband to the day of her own death, remained a widow in the utmost chastity.

How Ethelred and Alfred went to the Help of King Burhred.

In the same year the aforesaid army of the pagans departed from the Northumbrians and came into Mercia. And it reached Nottingham, which, being interpreted,

is in the British tongue Tigguocobauc, but in Latin
" speluncarum domus " ; and in that year the army
wintered in that place.   On the arrival of the heathen,
Burhred, king of the Mercians, and all the nobles of the
same people, forthwith sent messengers to Ethelred, king
of the West Saxons, and to Alfred, his brother, making
humble petition that they would come to their help, that
they might be able to fight with the said army ; and they
obtained their prayer with ease.   So those brothers, not
being slack in the performance of their promise, gathered
a great army from every side and entered Mercia, and
came in company as far as Nottingham, seeking battle.
And when the heathen, being safe in the protection of
the fortress, would not give battle, and when the
Christians could not break down the wall, peace was
made between the Mercians and the pagans, and those
two brothers, Ethelred and Alfred, returned home.

How the Pagans Ravaged England, and how
King Edmund Died.

A.D. 869.   In the year of the Incarnation of the Lord
eight hundred and sixty-nine, which was the twenty-first
from the birth of King Alfred, the same army of the
pagans rode again to Northumbria and reached the city of
York, where it stayed one whole year.

A.D. 870.   In the year of the Incarnation of the Lord

eight hundred and seventy, which was the twenty-first year
from the birth of King Alfred, the same army of the
pagans passed through Mercia into the land of the East
Angles, and there wintered in a place that is called
Thetford.

In the same year did Edmund, king of the East Angles,
fight fiercely against that army, but, sad to tell, the pagans
triumphed completely. And he, with the greater part of
his army, fell there, and the enemy held the place of
slaughter, and they subdued all that region under their
sway.

In the same year, Ceolnoth the priest, archbishop of
Canterbury, went the way of all flesh, and was buried in
peace in the same city.

How the Pagans Entered the Kingdom of the West Saxons.

A.D. 871. In the year of the Incarnation of the Lord
eight hundred and seventy-one, which was the twenty-
second year from the birth of King Alfred, the heathen
army, of hated memory, left the East Angles and entered
the kingdom of the West Saxons. It came to a royal
residence, Reading by name, which lies on the southern
bank of the river Thames, in the district which is called
Berkshire. And on the third day after it was come
thither, the leaders of the heathen, with a great part of

their host, rode forth to plunder, while the remainder digged a trench between the two rivers, the Thames and the Kennet, on the right-hand side of the said royal residence.

How the Christians Gained the Victory at Englefield.

Then did Ethelwulf, ealdorman of Berkshire, with his comrades, meet the pagans at a place that is called Englefield, and the battle was sternly waged on both sides. And when each army had long resisted, one of the pagan jarls was slain, and the greater part of the army was destroyed, and the remnant escaped by flight. So the Christians gained the victory and held the place of slaughter.

How the Heathen Beat the Saxons at Reading.

Then four days after these things had there happened, King Ethelred and Alfred, his brother, united their forces, and, when they had assembled an host, came to Reading. And when they advanced to the gates of the fortress, slaying and laying low all the heathen whom they found without the walls, then the pagans fought with energy, and rushed out of all the gates like wolves, and joined battle with all their might. There for a long while both sides fought bravely, but, alas! the Christians finally turned their backs, and the pagans gained the victory and held the

place of slaughter. There fell, among others, the said
Ethelwulf, the ealdorman.

How THE CHRISTIANS PREPARED FOR BATTLE AT ASHDOWN.

At this the Christians were moved with grief and shame,
and after four days, with all their strength and with a good
heart, they went forth to battle against the same army to
the place that is called Ashdown, which, being interpreted,
is in the Latin tongue " mons fraxini." But the pagans
divided their host into two bands of equal size and made
ready their shield-walls : for they had two kings and
many jarls, and they gave the centre of the army to the
two kings, and the rest to all the jarls. And when the
Christians saw this, they likewise divided their army into
two bands, and without delay formed their shield-walls.

How ALFRED CAME FIRST TO THE BATTLE.

But Alfred and his men, as we have heard from the
accounts of truth-telling eye-witnesses, came to the place
of battle the more rapidly and readily. For his brother,
King Ethelred, was still in his tent, praying fervently and
hearing Mass, and he stoutly declared that he would not
depart thence alive until the priest had made an end of
saying Mass. For he would not abandon the service of

God for that of man.   So did he, and the faith of this
Christian king availed much with the Lord, as will be
more clearly shown by that which follows.

How Alfred began the Battle of Ashdown.

Now the Christians had determined that King Ethelred,
with his forces, should undertake the battle against the
two pagan kings, but that Alfred, his brother, with his
forces, should know that he was to try the fortune of battle
against all the pagan jarls.   And when things had been so
fully ordered on each side, since the king remained too
long in prayer, and the pagans, being made ready, hastened
to the field of battle, Alfred, who was then second in
command, was unable longer to bear the attacks of the
enemy.   For it was needful that he should either retire
from the battle or enter into the conflict with the enemy's
host before the coming of his brother.   And at last, in
the manner of a wild boar, he led the Christian forces
boldly against the foe, as they had before determined, but
though the king was not yet come.   So, trusting in the
counsel of God, and confiding in His help, he drew his
shield-wall together in order, and forthwith advanced
against the enemy.

How the Christians Gained the Victory at Ashdown.

But here it must be made clear to those who know it not that the place of battle did not give equal advantage to each side since the pagans had already seized on the higher ground and the Christians made their attack uphill. There was, moreover, in that place a single very stunted thorn-tree, which we have ourselves beheld with our own eyes. Round about this tree, then, the hostile armies clashed together in battle, with loud cries on all sides, the one part supporting an evil cause, the other fighting for life, and their loved ones, and their native land. And when both sides had for some while fought everywhere with zeal and very fiercely, by the judgment of God, the heathen were no more able to withstand the onslaught of the Christians. And when the more part of their forces had been slain they turned in shameful flight.

In that place fell one of the two pagan kings, and five of their jarls were slain. And on all sides many thousand of the pagan host met their death there, and moreover their dead bodies were strewn over the whole breadth of the plain of Ashdown.

Then fell there Bacsecg the king, and Sidroc that old chieftain, and Sidroc the younger, and Osbern and Frena, and Harald, jarls. And to the fall of night and even to the following day the whole pagan army was driven in flight until they came to the fortress whence they had gone out. And the Christians pursued them until dark, and everywhere laid them low.

How the War Continued, and how King Ethelred Died.

When these things had thus befallen there, again after fourteen days, King Ethelred and Alfred, his brother, united their forces to fight against the heathen, and came to Basing. When battle had been joined on both sides, and had for a long while continued, the pagans gained the victory and held the place of slaughter. And after the battle was ended another pagan army came from the lands across the sea and joined itself to the host.

And in the same year, after Easter, the said King Ethelred, after that he had for five years, amid many tribulations, ruled the kingdom with ability and honour and in good fame, went the way of all flesh. And he was buried in the monastery of Wimborne, and awaits the Advent of the Lord and the first resurrection with the just.

How Alfred began to Reign.

In that year this same Alfred, who up to that time, while his brothers lived, had been the recognised heir to the throne, by a grant of divine providence and with the full assent of all the inhabitants of that land, at once upon the death of his brother received the rule of the whole realm. And even while that same brother yet lived, had he wished to receive it, he could most easily have obtained the government, with the assent of all men, since of a truth both in wisdom and in all good qualities he surpassed all his brothers, and moreover because he was very warlike and was victorious in almost every battle. He began to reign, then, as it were against his will, inasmuch as he did not think that it was within his power, trusting in the aid of God alone, ever to withstand such great fierceness of the heathen, since, while his brothers yet lived, he had suffered many and manifold trials.

How Alfred First Fought the Pagans After That he was Become King, and Concerning the Year of Battles.

Then, when he had reigned one full month, with a few men and an army of which the number was very unequal to the task, he contended with the whole host of the pagans on a hill named Wilton, lying on the southern bank of the river Wylye, wherefrom all that district takes its name. And when for no small part of the day the battle had been contested on both sides and in every part of the field fiercely and strenuously, the pagans with their own eyes perceived the full extent of their danger, and no longer bearing the ons'aught of their enemies, they turned and fled. But, alas! they deceived our men into rash pursuit, and again entering into the battle, they secured the victory and held the place of slaughter.

Nor need this cause wonder to any one, since the number of the Christians in that battle was small. For by the eight battles with the pagans in that one year, in the which one of the kings of the pagans, and nine chieftains, besides soldiers innumerable, had fallen, the Saxons were in general almost utterly worn out. And this takes no account of the countless attacks by day and by night which the oft-mentioned Alfred, and all the chief men of that people, with their followers, and very many of the king's thegns also, made upon the heathen, with zest and without wearying. And how many thousands of the pagan host were slain in these constant attacks, that is, who fell over and above those who fell in the eight battles already mentioned, is known to none save to God.

In this year also the Saxons made an agreement with the pagans on this condition that they should depart from them. This also the pagans did.

How the Pagans Ravaged all England.

A.D. 872. In the year of the Incarnation of the Lord eight hundred and seventy-two, which was the twenty-third from the birth of King Alfred, the same army of the pagans came to London and there passed the winter. And with it the Mercians made a peace.

A.D. 873. In the year of the Incarnation of the Lord eight hundred and seventy-three, which was the twenty-fourth from the birth of King Alfred, the oft-mentioned army left London and went into the land of the Northumbrians, and there it wintered in the district which is called Lindsey. And the Mercians again made a peace with it.

A. D. 874. In the year of the Incarnation of the Lord eight hundred and seventy-four, which was the twenty-fifth from the birth of King Alfred, the oft-mentioned army left Lindsey and entered Mercia, and it wintered at the place which is called Repton.

How King Burhred was Driven From his Kingdom.

The pagans also compelled Burhred, king of the Mercians, to abandon his kingdom and to depart over sea, and to go to Rome, against his will, in the twenty-second year of his reign. And he lived but short while after that he was come to Rome, and died there. He was buried with honour in the church of Saint Mary in the School of the Saxons, and awaits the Advent of the Lord and the first resurrection with the just.

Then after he had been driven out the pagans reduced all Mercia under their sway. Yet did they entrust it to the care of a certain foolish thegn of the king, Ceowulf by name, on these disgraceful terms, that if they wished at any time to have it again he should give them peaceable possession of it.   And for the fulfilment of these terms he gave hostages to them, and he swore that he would in nowise resist their will but would in all things be obedient to them.

How the Army of the Pagans was Divided.

A.D. 875.   In the year of the Incarnation of the Lord eight hundred and seventy-five, which was the twenty-sixth from the birth of King Alfred, the oft-mentioned army left Repton and was divided into two bands.   And the one part with Halfdene went into the land of the Northumbrians and there wintered near the river which is called Tyne.   And he subdued the whole land of the Northumbrians under his sway, and subdued the Picts also ; and the men of Strathclyde were cut short.

And the other part, with Guthrum and Oscytil and Amund, three kings of the pagans, went to the place called Cambridge and there passed the winter.

And in the same year King Alfred fought a battle with ships in the sea against six ships of the pagans, and he took one of them, the rest escaping by flight.

How the Pagans Broke Faith with Alfred and Went to Exeter.

A.D. 876.   In the year of the Incarnation of the Lord eight hundred and seventy-six, which was the twenty-seventh year from the birth of King Alfred, the oft-mentioned army of the pagans left Cambridge by night and entered a fortress which is called Wareham.   This is a monastery of nuns, lying between the rivers Frome and Trent, in the district which is called in the British tongue Durngueis, but in the Saxon Thornsaeta.   Now its situation is the safest in the world, except in respect of its western side where it is joined to the mainland.

With this army King Alfred made a sure agreement, upon condition that it should depart from him.   And the pagans without reluctance gave him hostages, whom he named for himself, swearing an oath upon all the relics in the which the king had most confidence after the Lord that with all speed they would depart out of his realm : and before this the army would not so swear to any nation. Yet, as was ever its custom, it acted deceitfully, and considered neither the hostages nor its oath, nor the faith which it had sworn.   For upon a certain night it broke the treaty, and dispatched all the horsemen that it had westwards into Devonshire, and made a sudden raid upon another place which is called in the Saxon tongue Exeter, but in the British Cairwisc, and in the Latin " civitas

Exae." This city lies on the eastern bank of the river Wisc, and near the southern sea which flows between Gaul and Britain. There the army wintered.

In the same year also Halfdene, king of that part, meted out the whole land of the Northumbrians to himself and to his men; and he and his men began to cultivate that land.

How Rollo Entered Normandy.

In the same year Rollo, with his men, entered Normandy. This same Rollo, while with his army he wintered in old Britain or England, one night enjoyed a vision of that which was soon surely to come to pass. And of this Rollo more may be seen in the Annals.

How Alfred Caused Ships to be Built, and how the Pagans were Beaten at Swanage.

A.D. 877. In the year of the Incarnation of the Lord eight hundred and seventy-seven, as autumn drew nigh, some of the pagans remained at Exeter, and some returned to Mercia in search of plunder. Moreover the number of the heathen increased every day, so that, indeed, if thirty thousand of them were slain in one day, twice that number would take their place. At that time did King Alfred command barks and galleys, that is, long ships, to be built throughout his dominions, that he might engage in a naval battle with those who were newly arriving. In them he placed pirates, and gave them charge to protect the ways of the sea.

But he himself hastened to Exeter, where the pagans were then wintering, and when he had shut them in, he laid siege to the city. Moreover he gave orders to his sailors that they should suffer no great assistance to come to the enemy by way of the estuary. Then there met with his sailors an hundred and twenty ships filled with armed men, who were coming to the help of their comrades; and when the king's officers knew that the ships were filled with heathen they rushed to arms and boldly attacked the barbarous nations. But the pagans, who had now for almost a month suffered disaster amid the waves of the wild sea, fought against them in vain. Therefore in the twinkling of an eye were their ranks broken, and they were swallowed up in the waters, and they all perished together at a place which is called Swanage.

In the same year the army of the heathen left Wareham, some on horseback and some in ships. And when they came to the place called Swanage an hundred and twenty of the ships were lost. But then King Alfred followed the army that was on horseback until it came to Exeter. There he took hostages and an oath from the pagans that they should depart forthwith.

How the Pagans Divided Mercia.

In the month of August in that same year the army went into Mercia. They gave part of the land of the

Mercians to Ceolwulf, a certain foolish thegn of the king, and part divided they among themselves.

How the Pagans Came to Chippenham.

A.D. 878.   In the year of the Incarnation of the Lord eight hundred and seventy-eight, which was the twenty-seventh year from the birth of King Alfred, the same oft-mentioned army left Exeter and came to Chippenham, a royal residence lying in the left-hand part of Wiltshire and on the eastern bank of that river which in the British tongue is called Abon.   There it passed the winter. And the pagans drove many of that nation by force, and poverty and fear, to sail over sea, and they subdued almost all the dwellers in that region under their sway.

How Alfred abode in Athelney.

In those days King Alfred, whom we have so often mentioned above, with a few of his nobles and with some soldiers and vassals also, passed his life in great sorrow and unrest amid the woods and marshes of the land of Somerset.   Nor had he anything wherewith to support life, save that which by constant raids, either secretly or openly, he might take from the pagans, and from the Christians even, who had submitted to the pagan yoke.

The Story of the Burning of the Cakes.

And in the life of the holy father Neot may be read that which chanced to him in the hut of one of his cowherds.

For it fell out upon a certain day that the poor woman, the wife of that cowherd, made ready cakes for the baking, and the king was sitting by the hearth, preparing his bow and arrows and other weapons of war. But when the wretched woman saw the cakes, which she had set near the fire, burning, she ran in hastily and moved them, abusing the unconquered king, and saying, " Ah, you man! when you saw the cakes burning, why were you too lazy to turn them ? For you are glad enough to eat them all hot." Now that unlucky woman little thought that he was King Alfred, who fought so many battles against the pagans and gained so many victories over them.

How Alfred Merited his Misfortunes.

Yet the Lord did not think to grant to that glorious king only victory over his enemies and prosperity in adversity. But, indeed, the same good God many times suffered him to be wearied by his enemies, to be troubled with ill-fortune, and to be shamed in the sight of his own men, that he might know that there is one Lord of all, to Whom every knee shall bow, in Whose hand are the hearts of kings, Who puts down the mighty from their seats and exalteth the humble, Who willeth

*that those who are faithful to Him, when they are set in great
honour, should sometimes feel the scourgings of evil fortune, that
when they are brought low, they should not despair of the
mercy of God, and when they are exalted, they should not
glory in their honour; but that they should know to Whom
they owe all things, whatsoever they have.*

*Now indeed we believe that this ill-fortune came not upon
that king contrary to his deserts. For when he began to
reign, as he was yet a young man, he was given up to youthful passions, and when the men of the realm subject to him
came to him and sought his aid and favour, he would neither
hear them nor give any help to them, but utterly despised
them.*

*At this also the most holy Neot, who was still abiding in the
flesh, and who was his relative, was cut to the heart, and, being
filled with the spirit of prophecy, foretold that for this cause
great adversity would come upon him. But the king cared
little for the most just correction of the man of God, and did
not receive his true prophecy. Wherefore, inasmuch as every
sin of man must be punished in some manner, either in this life
or in that which is to come, the true and righteous Judge would
not that the folly of the king should go unpunished in this
world, that He might spare him in the last judgment. For
this cause, then, did the oft-mentioned Alfred fall many times
into so great misfortune, that none of his subjects knew where
he was or what had befallen him.*

How the Pagans were beaten in North Devon.

In the same year the brother of Ingwar and Halfdene, with twenty-three ships, after that he had made great slaughter of the Christians in Dyfed, where he had passed the winter, sailed away to Devonshire. And there, while he was working mischief, he came to a sad end and was slain by the king's thegns before the fortress of Cynwit, and a thousand and two hundred men with him: for many thegns of the king, with their men, had taken refuge in the same fortress. But when the heathen saw that the fortress was ill-prepared and altogether unfortified, as it had only walls made after our fashion, yet they did not try to break into it. For that place, owing to the character of its situation, is very safe on all sides except the eastern, as we have ourselves seen. Then they began to besiege it, thinking that those men would soon give way to hunger and thirst and be overcome by the siege, since there was no water near that fortress. But it fell not out as they expected. For the Christians, rather than endure such distress at all, and being prompted from on high, deemed it far better either to suffer death or to gain the victory. And at dawn of day they suddenly rushed forth against the pagans, and at the first attack they slew most of the enemy, with their king, a few escaping by fleeing to their ships.

How The Raven Banner was Taken.

And there took they no small spoil, and in that battle they took also the standard which they call The Raven. Now it is told that the three sisters of Ingwar and Hubba, the daughters of Lodbrok, weaved that banner and completed it entirely between dawn and dusk on a single day. Moreover they say that in every battle in which that banner goes before them, the raven in the midst of the design seems to flutter as though it were alive, if they were destined to gain the day ; but and if they were about to be conquered in the coming fight, it would droop down without moving : and this has often been proved to be true.

How Alfred came forth from Athelney.

In the same year, after Eastertide, King Alfred, with a few men, made a fort in a place that is called Athelney, and from this fort, with the chief men of Somerset, he constantly attacked the heathen, without wearying. And again in the seventh week after Easter he rode to Egbert's Stone, which is in the eastern part of the wood which is called Selwood, but in the Latin tongue " Sylva Magna," and in the British Coitmawr.

And there met him at that place all the people of the districts of Somerset and Wiltshire, and all the people of the land of Hampshire, who had not gone beyond the sea for fear of the pagans. When they saw the king, as was right, they received him after so great tribulation as one risen from the dead, and they were filled with joy unspeakable. There they encamped one night.

How Alfred came to Edington and beat the Pagans there.

And when the next day was now dawning the king moved his camp thence and came to the place which is called Aecglea, and there camped for one night. And at dawn on the following day he set his standards in motion and came to the place called Edington. And he fought fiercely against the whole host of the pagans, forming his shield-wall closely, and striving long and boldly. And at the last, by God's help, he gained the victory, and with great slaughter overthrew the pagans, and smiting the fugitives, pursued them to the fort. And all things, men and horses and beasts, that he found without the fort he took, and the men he slew forthwith.

How the Pagans submitted to King Alfred, and how King Guthrum was made Christian.

Then he boldly pitched his camp, with all his host, before the gates of the pagan fortress. And when he had abode there fourteen days the pagans were overcome by hunger and cold and fear, and at the last despaired. Then

they sought peace on these terms that the king should
receive from them hostages, as many as he would, and
that he should give no hostage to them; and never,
indeed, had they made peace with any one on the like
terms.   And when he had heard their embassy the king
was moved with pity and received from them chosen
hostages, as many as he desired; and after they had been
received the pagans also swore that they would straightway depart from his realm. Moreover Guthrum, their king,
in addition promised that he would accept Christianity and
would receive baptism at the hand of King Alfred.

And he and his men performed all these things as they
had promised.   For after seven weeks Guthrum, the
king of the pagans, with thirty of the most chosen men of
his army, came to King Alfred at a place called Aller,
near to Athelney, and King Alfred received him as his
son by adoption and raised him from the holy font of
baptism.   And his chrism-loosing was on the eighth day,
at the royal residence which is called Wedmore.   And
after that he was baptised he remained twelve nights with
the king, and to him and to all his men the king gave
freely many and excellent articles of goldsmiths' work.

How the Pagans left the land of the West Saxons.

A.D. 879. In the year of the Incarnation of the Lord
eight hundred and seventy-nine, which was the twenty-

eighth year from the birth of King Alfred, the same pagan army, departing from Chippenham, as they had promised, went to Cirencester, which is called in the British tongue Cairceri, and which is in the south part of the land of the Hwiccas. There it remained one year.

In the same year an army of the pagans sailed from the lands across the sea and came into the river Thames, and joined the former army. Yet it passed the winter in a place near to the river Thames, Fulham by name.

And in this year there was an eclipse of the sun, between nones and vespers, but nearer to nones.

A.D. 880. In the year of the Incarnation of the Lord eight hundred and eighty, which was the twenty-ninth year from the birth of King Alfred, the oft-mentioned army of the pagans left Cirencester and went into the land of the East Angles, and meting out that region began to dwell therein.

In the same year the army of the pagans which had passed the winter at Fulham left the island of Britain, and sailed again across the sea, and came to East Francia, and remained one year in the place that is called Ghent.

How the Heathen warred in the land of the Franks, and how Alfred beat them at Sea.

A.D. 881. In the year of the Incarnation of the Lord eight hundred and eighty-one, which was the thirtieth year from the birth of King Alfred, the same army went farther into the land of the Franks, and the Franks fought against it, and when the battle was ended the pagans found horses and became horsemen.

A.D. 882. In the year of the Incarnation of the Lord eight hundred and eighty-two, which was the thirty-first year from the birth of King Alfred, the same army drew its ships up the river which is called Meuse and went much farther into Francia, and there wintered for one year.

And in the same year Alfred, king of the Anglo-Saxons, fought a battle with ships in the sea against the pagan ships, and he took two of them and slew all who were in them. And the two commanders of two other ships, with all their comrades, being much wearied with the battle and with their wounds, laid down their arms, and, with bended knee and suppliant prayers, gave themselves up to the king.

A.D. 883. In the year of the Incarnation of the Lord eight hundred and eighty-three, which was the thirty-second year from the birth of King Alfred, the same army steering their ships against the stream, drew them by the river which is called Scheldt to a monastery of nuns, called Condé, and there remained one year.

How the Pagans Attacked Rochester in Vain.

A.D. 884.   In the year of the Incarnation of the Lord eight hundred and eighty-four, which was the thirty-third year from the birth of King Alfred, the same army divided into two bands.   One band went into East Francia, and the other came to Britain.   And when it had reached Kent it laid siege to the town which is called in the Saxon tongue Rochester and which lies on the eastern bank of the river Medway.   Before the gate of this place the pagans at once built a strong fortress, and yet they were unable to take that city, since the citizens valiantly defended themselves, until King Alfred, bearing help to them, came with a great army.

Then the pagans left their fortress and abandoned all the horses which they had brought with them out of the land of the Franks, and moreover they left the greater number of their prisoners in the fort, owing to the sudden coming of the king, and at once fled to their ships.   And the Saxons straightway seized the prisoners and the horses which had been abandoned by the pagans.   Therefore the pagans, compelled by stern necessity, in the same summer went again to Francia.

How Alfred sent his Fleet against East Anglia.

In the same year Alfred, king of the Anglo-Saxons, sent his fleet filled with warriors from Kent and dispatched it to the land of the East Angles to take booty. And when they had come to the mouth of the river Stour, forthwith thirteen ships of the pagans made ready for battle, met with them, and a naval battle was begun and they fought boldly on either side. Then all the pagans were slain, and all their ships and treasure taken.

And when the victorious fleet of the king was now about to return home, the pagans dwelling in the land of the East Angles, having gathered ships from every quarter, met the same royal fleet at the mouth of the same river. And when a naval battle had been joined the pagans had the victory.

CONCERNING THE AFFAIRS OF THE FRANKISH KINGDOM.

In this year also a wild boar attacked Carloman, king of the West Franks, as he was hunting boars, and, tearing him with its savage tusk, brought him to a terrible death. His brother Lewis had died in the previous year, having himself also been king of the Franks: for they were both sons of Lewis, king of the Franks. This Lewis moreover died in the year mentioned above, in the which there was an eclipse of the sun, and he himself was the son of Charles, king of the Franks, whose daughter, Judith, Ethelwulf, king of the West Saxons, received as his queen, with the assent of her father.

In the same year also a great army of the pagans went

from Germany into the land of the Old Saxons, which in the Saxon tongue is called Ealdseaxum. Against them, the same Saxons and the Frisians, having united their armies, fought valiantly there and in that one year. And in these two battles, by the help of the divine pity, the Christians gained the victory.

And in the same year Charles, king of the Alamanni, with the free assent of all men, received the kingdom of the East Franks, and all the kingdoms which lie between the Mediterranean Sea and that arm of the ocean which lies between the Old Saxons and the Gauls, with the exception of the kingdom of Armorica. This Charles was the son of King Lewis, who was brother to Charles, king of the Franks, that is, to the father of the said Queen Judith. They twain were the sons of Lewis, who was the son of Charles, who was the son of Pippin.

Concerning Pope Marinus.

In this same year Pope Marinus, of blessed memory, went the way of all flesh. He, of his kindness, and for his love towards Alfred, king of the Anglo-Saxons, and at his prayer, freed the School of the Saxons abiding in Rome, from all tribute and customary payment. Moreover he sent back many gifts to the same king, and among those things which he gave him there was also no small portion of the most holy and revered cross on which

Our Lord Jesus Christ hung for the salvation of all men.

How the Pagans of East Anglia broke the Peace.

It was in this year, too, that the army of the pagans, which dwelt in the land of the East Angles, shamefully broke the peace which it had made with King Alfred.

How the Author Returns to the Account of the Life and Character of King Alfred.

And so let me return to that point from which I have departed, lest, by long voyaging, I be driven to lose the longed-for haven of rest. I will undertake to set forth what little has come to my knowledge concerning the life and manners and good conversation of my Lord Alfred, king of the Anglo-Saxons. I will tell also not a little of the deeds which he wrought from the time when he wedded that revered wife of the race of the nobles of Mercia. And this, with God's help, I will do shortly and in brief, as I have promised, lest by the long telling of each fact I offend the minds of those who are difficult to satisfy.

How Alfred fell Ill at the Time of his Wedding.

Therefore, while he was celebrating his wedding in Mercia, with honour and with pomp, and in the presence of a countless throng of men and women, and after long feasting by day and night, forthwith he was taken by a sudden and severe pain before all the people. Nor was this illness known to any of the physicians, for it was beyond the skill of all who were then present and also of all who have seen it from that day to this. And, alas! that which is worst is that, during so many years, from the twentieth year of his age to the fortieth, and even longer, it should have continued, without ceasing, through so many passing years from the time when it began.

Now many considered that this came to pass owing to the applause and devotion of the people who stood round; others, that it came from the hatred of the devil who is ever hostile to the righteous. There were some who thought it to be the result of an unusual form of fever, and others who regarded it as being the ficus.

Concerning the Earlier Illnesses of Alfred.

Now this last most evil form of illness he had endured from infancy. But some while before, by the inspiration of God, he had gone to Cornwall to hunt, and had turned aside to pray at a certain church where Saint Gueryr rests, and where Saint Neot now also reposes. For he was also from childhood a constant seeker of the shrines of saints, for the sake of prayer and for the giving of alms. There he remained long prostrate in silent prayer, and so sought the mercy of the Lord, that

Almighty God, in His wondrous pity, would be pleased to change the pains of this present and hateful affliction for some other lighter misfortune, but such that his illness should not appear without, lest he might be useless and despised. For he feared leprosy and blindness, which soon make the man upon whom they fall useless and despised.

Then when he had ended his prayer he set out on the journey which he had begun, and not long afterwards, as he had sought in his prayer, he felt himself divinely healed of that ill, so that it was utterly rooted out. Yet he had obtained this ill also as a pious suppliant in the first flower of his youth, after earnest prayer and frequent petitions to God.

For that I may say something shortly and in a few words, though out of due course, concerning the ardent devotion of his mind to God, when he was in the first flower of his youth, before he had a wife of his own, he wished to keep his mind firm in the commandments of God. And he saw that he could not be free from carnal desires, and feared that he would merit the anger of God if he did anything contrary to His will. Very often, therefore, he rose in secret at cockcrow, and in the morning hours, and sought the churches and the relics of saints for the sake of prayer, and prostrating himself there for a long while he prayed that Almighty God, of His mercy, would strengthen him and turn him wholly to Him, making his mind more ardent in the love of service to Him, by means of some infirmity, which he might be able to bear, and yet which should not make him unworthy or useless in earthly matters. And when he so did many times with great devotion of soul, after some short space of time, by the gift of God, he obtained the same illness of the ficus, in which he laboured long and painfully for many years, and even despaired of life, until at his prayer it was utterly taken from him. But, alas! after it had been taken away, another worse ill took him, as we have said, at the time of his marriage, and this unceasingly afflicted him from the twentieth year of his age until his forty-fifth, day and night.

But if at any time, through the mercy of God, that infirmity was taken from him for a day or a night, or even for the space oj one hour, still the fear and dread of that terrible pain never left him, but it made him, as it seemed to him, nearly useless, as it were, in things divine and human.

CONCERNING THE FAMILY OF KING ALFRED.

Now there were born to him by the said wife, sons and daughters. And first came Ethelfleda, the first-born, and after her Edward, and then Elgiva, and then Elftryth, and then Ethelward, besides those whom an early death took away in infancy, among the number of whom was Edmund.

Ethelfleda, when the time for her marriage came, was wedded to Edred, ealdorman of the Mercians. Elgiva entered the service of God, and was wedded and conse-

crated to God, and devoted to Him as a virgin, under the
rule of the monastic life.

Ethelward, the youngest of all, through the counsel of
God and by the great forethought of the king, was given
up, under the watchful care of masters, to the pleasures of
the discipline of letters, in company with almost all the
children of noble birth in the whole realm and even of
many of lower birth. And in this school books in both
tongues, that is, in Latin and in Saxon, were zealously
read, and they had leisure for writing. Therefore, before
they had the strength for manly pursuits, such as hunting,
and other arts which befit nobles, they became eager and
skilled in the liberal arts.

Edward and Elftryth were always brought up in the
royal court with great care by the men and women who
had charge of their upbringing. And, indeed, to this day
they remain there amid the love of all, showing kind
humility towards all, whether born in the land or strangers,
and mercy, and steadfast obedience to their father. Nor
are they allowed by slackness and want of care to be
without a liberal education among the other occupations
of this life which are becoming to nobles. For they have
carefully learned both the psalms and Saxon books, and
especially Saxon poems, and they use books very often.

How Alfred Cared for the Good of his Realm.

Yet amid the wars and many hindrances of this present life, and amid the assaults of the pagans, and his daily illness, the king ceased not from the governance of the kingdom and from the pursuit of every form of hunting. Nor did he omit to instruct also his goldsmiths and all his artificers, his falconers and his huntsmen and the keepers of his dogs ; nor to make according to new designs of his own articles of goldsmiths' work, more venerable and more precious than had been the wont of all his predecessors. He was constant in the reading of books in the Saxon tongue, and more especially in committing to memory the Saxon poems, and in commanding others to do so. And he by himself laboured most zealously with all his might.

Concerning the Virtues of Alfred.

Moreover he heard the divine offices daily, the Mass, and certain psalms and prayers. He observed the services of the hours by day and by night, and oftentimes was he wont, as we have said, without the knowledge of his men, to go in the night-time to the churches for the sake of prayer. He was zealous in the giving of alms, and generous towards his own people and to those who came from all nations. He was especially and wonderfully kindly towards all men, and merry. And to the searching out of things not known did he apply himself with all his heart.

Moreover many Franks, Frisians and Gauls, pagans, Britons, Scots and Armoricans, of their own free will, submitted them to his rule, both nobles and persons of low degree. All these he ruled, according to his excellent goodness, as he did his own people, and loved them and honoured them, and enriched them with money and with power.

He was eager and anxious to hear the Holy Scripture read to him by his own folk, but he would also as readily pray with strangers, if by any chance one had come from any place. Moreover he loved with wonderful affection his bishops and all the clergy, his ealdormen and nobles, his servants and all his household. And cherishing their sons, who were brought up in the royal household, with no less love than he bore towards his own children, he ceased not day and night, among other things, himself to teach them all virtue and to make them well acquainted with letters.

How the King Desired Wisdom.

But it was as though he found no comfort in all these things. For, as if he suffered no other care from within or without, in anxious sorrow, day and night, he would make complaint to the Lord and to all who were joined to him in close affection, lamenting with many sighs for that Almighty God had not made him skilled in divine wisdom and in the liberal arts.   In this he resembled the pious and most wise and rich Solomon, king of the Hebrews, who, despising all the glory and riches of this world, sought first wisdom from God, and so found both, that is, wisdom and the glory of this world, as it is written, Seek ye first the kingdom of God and his righteousness, and all these things shall be added unto you.

Now it is God Who ever regards the inmost thoughts, Who prompts our thoughts and all good desires, Who mercifully grants that good desires may be obtained, and Who causes a man to desire the good only when He also bountifully provides that which any man well and rightly desires to have.   He, then, stirred up the mind of the king by inward working, as it is written, I will hearken what the Lord God will say concerning me.

How the King Sought Helpers.

He would obtain, whencesoever he could, those who might assist his righteous intention and who might be able to aid him in acquiring the wisdom for which he longed, whereby he should gain his passionate desire.   As the prudent bee in time of summer leaves the cells that it loves at dawn of day, and steers its course, swiftly flying, through

the unknown ways of the air, and pitches upon many and
divers blooms of herbs and plants and fruits, finding that
which best pleases it and bearing it home, so the king
turned the gaze of his mind afar and sought from abroad
that which he had not at home, that is, in his own
kingdom.

How the King Obtained Helpers from Mercia.

But then God sent some comfort to the good-will of
the king, no longer suffering so righteous and just a complaint to continue, and He gave him, as it were, certain
lights. For He gave to him Werferth, who was bishop
of the church of Worcester, and who was well learned in
the Holy Scriptures. He it was who, by the command
of the king, clearly and beautifully translated the books of
the Dialogues of Pope Gregory with Peter, his disciple,
for the first time, from the Latin tongue into the Saxon,
sometimes making a paraphrase. Then He sent Plegmund, a Mercian by nation, archbishop of the church of
Canterbury, a reverend man and one endued with wisdom ;
and Athelstan also, and Werwulf, priests and chaplains,
Mercians by race, learned men. These four did King
Alfred call to him out of Mercia, and exalted them with
many honours and much power in the kingdom of the
West Saxons, over and above that which Archbishop
Plegmund and Bishop Werferth had in Mercia.

From the teaching and wisdom of all these men the desire of the king was ever inflamed, and grew greater. For day and night, and whenever he had any leisure, he commanded such men to read books before him, nor would he ever suffer himself to be without one of them. And for this cause he had knowledge of almost all books, though as yet he was not able of himself to understand anything from the books, for he had still not begun to read anything.

How Grimbald and John the Old Saxon Came to the King.

But the royal greed, which was yet worthy of praise, in this matter was still unsated. And he sent messengers beyond the sea into Gaul to fetch masters, and summoned thence Grimbald, a priest and monk, a reverend man, an excellent singer, and very learned in every kind of ecclesiastical discipline and in the Holy Scriptures, and adorned with every good quality. And he summoned John, who was also a priest and a monk, a man of very cunning mind, and very learned in all the rules of the art of letters, and skilled in many other arts. By their teaching the mind of the king was much enlarged, and he enriched them with great power, and honoured them.

How Asser Came to the King.

In those days also was I summoned by the king, and I came to him into the land of the Saxons from the western and uttermost parts of Britain. And when I had purposed to come to him through vast tracts of country, I arrived in the land of the right-hand Saxons, which in the Saxon tongue is called Suth-seaxum, being led on my way by guides of the same race. And there saw I him first, at the royal residence which is called Dean.

How Asser made an Agreement with the King.

And when I had been kindly received by him, amid the interchange of our opinions, he begged me earnestly to give myself up to his service and to become one of his household, and for his sake to leave all that I had in the land to the left-hand and west of the Severn. And he promised that he would return to me all those things and more besides, which also he has done.

Then I answered, "I cannot promise so much without thought, and rashly. For I think it not right for me to leave those most holy places in the which I was brought up and taught, where I received the tonsure, and at the last was ordained, for any earthly honour and power, unless by force and under compulsion."

To this he replied, "If it be not possible for you to

grant this, yet at least give me half of your service, so that for six months you may be with me and for the same space of time in Britain."

And to this I replied after this fashion, " I am not able lightly and rashly to promise this without taking counsel with my people." But yet, since I found that he desired my service, though for what cause I knew not, I promised that if my life were spared I would return again to him at the end of six months, with such answer as should be good for me and my people, and pleasing to him. And when this answer seemed good to him, and after I had given pledge that I would return at the appointed time, I rode from him on the fourth day and returned to my own land.

How Asser fell Ill, and how he Returned to the King.

But after my parting from him, a severe fever took me in the city of Winchester, and in that sickness I laboured day and night, with no hope of life, and unceasingly, for twelve months and a week. And when I came not to him at the appointed time, as I had promised, he sent letters to me, which urged me to ride to him and which sought for the cause of my delay. But, as I could not ride to him, I sent another letter to him, which made clear to him the occasion of my tarrying, and which

declared that if I could recover from that illness I would
fulfil that which I had promised.

Therefore, when the sickness had departed, by the
advice and permission of all my people, for the advantage
of that holy place, and of all the inhabiters thereof, as I
had promised to the king, I gave myself up to his service
so that I should spend six months in every year with him.
And if I were able, I should spend six months at one
time with him, or otherwise in two parts, so that I should
dwell for three months in Britain and for three months
in the land of the Saxons. And the former should win
help in every matter, through the efforts of Saint David,
as far as might be. For my people were hopeful that if I
were to come to the knowledge of that king, and to gain
his friendship, they would suffer lighter tribulations and
fewer injuries at the hand of King Hemeid.

Concerning the Affairs of Wales.

For Hemeid oftentimes wasted that monastery and the
see of Saint David, and sometimes drove out the bishops
who held the rule therein, as also at one time among the
same he drove out Archbishop Nobis, my relative, and
myself. In those days, then, and for a long while before,
all the lands of the right-hand part of Britain belonged to
King Alfred, and they still belong to him, since Hemeid,
with all the inhabitants of the land of Demetia, being

oppressed by the might of the six sons of Rhodri, had submitted themselves to his royal authority. Moreover Howell ap Rhys, king of Glewissig, and Brochmail and Fernmail, sons of Mouric, kings of Gwent, being driven by the might and tyranny of Edred the ealdorman and of the Mercians, of their own accord begged the same king that they might have governance and protection from him by reason of their enemies. And Helised ap Teudyr, king of Brecheiniog, oppressed by the might of the same sons of Rhodri, freely sought the lordship of the same king.

Last of all Anaraut ap Rhodri, also, with his brethren, abandoned the friendship of the Northumbrians, whence they had gained no good but hurt only, and sought earnestly for the friendship of the same king, and came into his presence. And when he had been received with honour by the king, and had been taken by him as his son from the hand of the bishop at confirmation, and had been enriched with very great gifts, he submitted to the rule of the king with all his people, in the same manner as did Ethelred and the Mercians, that is, so that he would in all things be obedient to the royal will.

Nor was it a vain thing that all these gained when they obtained the friendship of the king. For those who desired increase in their earthly power found it: those who desired wealth, received wealth: those who wished for friendship, obtained freindship: and those who desired

both, obtained both.   All, moreover, had love and care
and protection on every side, as far as the king could with
all his people defend himself.

How Asser abode with the King, and of the Gifts that the King gave Him.

Therefore when I had come to him at the royal
residence which is called Leonaford, I was honourably
received by him, and on that occasion I remained at the
court with him for eight months.   In that time I read to
him whatsoever books he would and which we had at
hand.   For it was his own most frequent custom day and
night, amid all his other cares of mind and body, either
to repeat the contents of books himself or to listen to
others doing so.   And when I often sought permission
from him to go home, I could in nowise obtain it.

Then at last, when I had resolved to demand leave
absolutely, at dusk on the eve of the day of the Nativity
of the Lord, I was summoned to him.   And he handed
to me two letters, in which was a detailed account of all
things which were in two monasteries, called, in the
Saxon tongue, Congresbury and Banwell.   On the same
day he gave to me those two monasteries with all that
was in them, and a pall of silk most precious, and as
much incense as could be borne by a strong man.   And
he added these words, " I do not give you these small

things because I will not in time come to give you greater gifts."

And, indeed, as time went on, he gave to me, to my surprise, Exeter, with the whole see thereof in the land of the Saxons and in Cornwall, in addition to countless daily gifts of all manner of earthly goods, which it would be tedious to mention here, lest that should cause weariness to those who read. But let none think that it is from any vain glory, or in flattery, or from a desire for gaining greater honour, that I have called to mind so many gifts in this place. For I witness before God that not for such cause have I done this, but that I might make clear to those who know it not how bountiful is his generosity.

Then forthwith he gave me leave to ride to those two monasteries, which were filled with all things good, and thence to return to my own land.

How the Pagans Besieged Paris in Vain.

A.D. 886. In the year of the Incarnation of the Lord eight hundred and eighty-six, which was the thirty-fifth year from the birth of Alfred, the oft-mentioned army again fled from the land and went into the country of the West Franks. And making their way into the river called Seine, they steered far up it against the stream and came to the city of Paris, and wintered there. They also made for themselves a camp at a bend in the river, near to the bridge, that they might prevent the citizens from crossing the bridge.   For that city is built on a little island in the midst of the river.   Then all that year they besieged that city, but, by the merciful favour of God, and through the valiant defence of the citizens, they were not able to break through the fortifications.

How Alfred Restored London.

In the same year Alfred, king of the Anglo-Saxons, honourably restored the city of London and made it habitable, after the burnings of cities and the slaughter of people.   And he handed it over to the care of his son-in-law, Ethelred, ealdorman of the Mercians.

To this king all the Angles and Saxons, who had before been scattered on every side, or who had been in captivity with the pagans, turned them of their own accord and submitted themselves to his rule.

Concerning Grimbald and the Men of Oxford.

In the same year there arose at Oxford a most evil and shameful contention between Grimbald and those most learned men, whom he had taken thither with him, and the former scholars whom he found there.   For the latter at his coming almost all refused to adopt the rules and methods and manner

*of teaching, which had been established by the same Grimbald.
For three years there was no great dissension between them,
but there was secret hatred that was clear as the light, and
which afterwards burst forth with very great violence.*

*And that he might calm this, the unconquered King Alfred,
who had been informed of the discord by the messenger, and
complaint of Grimbald, went to Oxford to put an end to and
to settle this controversy. And he in person engaged in great
toil in hearing the arguments and complaints of each side. Now
the origin of this dispute consisted in this, that the old scholars
contended that before Grimbald came to Oxford, letters
flourished there abundantly, though now the scholars were fewer
in number than in earlier times, very many having been
driven away by the fierceness and tyranny of the heathen.
But they proved and showed by the undoubted witness of
ancient annals that the ordinances and institutions of that
place had been sanctioned by many holy and learned men, as
by holy Gildas, Melkin, Nennius and Kentigern, and others,
all of whom had studied letters there, arranging all things in
that place in peace and concord. And they said that Saint
Germanus also had come to Oxford, and had remained there
for half a year, at the time when he journeyed through
Britain preaching against the heresy of the Pelagians, and
had approved very greatly of their ordinances and institutions.
The king heard each side with wonderful humility, and in
detail, again and again urging them with pious and salutary*

advice to preserve general harmony and concord with one another.

So the king departed, thinking that on both sides they would obey his counsel and keep his commands. But Grimbald was angered at this, and forthwith went to the monastery which had been lately founded by Alfred at Winchester, and then took care to remove to Winchester the tomb in which he intended his bones to be laid to rest after the course of this life was completed, in the crypt which had been made under the chancel of the church of Saint Peter in Oxford. And, indeed, this church Grimbald had himself built, with great care and of polished stones, from the very foundations.

How the Pagans Warred in the Land of the West Franks.

A.D. 887. In the year of the Incarnation of the Lord eight hundred and eighty-seven, which was the thirty-sixth year from the birth of King Alfred, the above-mentioned army of the pagans left the city of Paris safe, and, since they had no other way in which to profit themselves, they rowed their fleet under the bridge and went a long way against the current of the Seine and journeyed for a long while until they came to the mouth of the river which is called Marne. Then they left the Seine and entered the mouth of the Marne and steered up

it for a long while and to a great distance, and at last, not
without toil, came to the place called Chézy, which is a
royal residence.   There they wintered for a whole year.
In the next year they entered the mouth of the river
called Yonne, to the great hurt of that region, and
remained there for one year.

CONCERNING KING ARNULF.

In the same year Charles, king of the Franks, went
the way of all flesh, but Arnulf, his brother's son, in the
sixth week before his death, had driven him from that
kingdom.   And as soon as Charles was dead five kings
were ordained, and the realm was divided into five parts.
None the less the chief seat of the kingdom passed to
Arnulf, rightly and deservedly, if it had not been for the
shameful wrong which he did against his uncle.   The
other four kings promised faith and obedience to Arnulf,
as was fitting, for none of these four kings had hereditary
right to that kingdom on the father's side, save Arnulf
alone.   Therefore five kings were ordained as soon as
Charles was on the point of death, but the empire remained
in the hands of Arnulf.

After such manner, then, was that realm divided :
Arnulf received the lands east of the river Rhine, and
Rudolf, the interior of the kingdom, and Odo, the western
kingdom.   Berengar and Guido received Lombardy, to-

gether with those regions which are in that part of the mountains. Yet did they not keep so many and great realms with peace among themselves, for they fought two battles against each other and very often laid those realms waste in turn, and one drove the other from the kingdom.

How Alfred sent Alms to Rome.

In the same year also in which the pagan army left the city of Paris and came to Chézy, Ethelhelm, ealdorman of Wiltshire, bore the alms of King Alfred and of the Saxons to Rome.

How Alfred's Handbook was begun.

In the same year also the oft-mentioned Alfred, king of the Anglo-Saxons, by the inspiration of God, began first to read and to interpret at the same time on one and the same day. But that the matter may be quite clear to those who know it not, I will take care to explain the reason for this late beginning.

For when we were one day sitting together in the royal chamber and were holding converse upon divers topics, as our wont was, it chanced that I repeated to him a quotation from a certain book. And when he had listened attentively to this with all his ears, and had carefully pondered it in the deep of his mind, suddenly he showed

me a little book, which he carried constantly in the fold
of his cloak. In it were written the Daily Course, and
certain psalms, and some prayers, which he had read in
his youth, and he commanded that I should write that
quotation in the same little book.

When I heard this, and knew in part his willing mind
and his zealous devotion towards the study of the wisdom
of God, I raised my hands to heaven and gave great
thanks, though in silence, to Almighty God, Who had
put such zeal for the study of wisdom in the royal heart.
But I found no empty space in that same book in the
which I might write that quotation, since it was altogether
filled with many matters. Therefore I hesitated for a little
while, for this cause most of all that I was eager to pro-
voke the excellent understanding of the king to a greater
knowledge of the witness of God.

And when he urged me to write that as quickly as possible, I said to him, " Are you willing that I should write
that quotation apart by itself on some small leaf? For
we know not that at some time we shall not find some
other such quotation, or more than one, which will please
you : and if it should so turn out unexpectedly, we
shall rejoice that we have kept this apart from the
rest."

And when he heard this, he said, " Your counsel is
good." And I, hearing this and being glad, made ready
a book of several leaves, in haste, and at the beginning of

it I wrote that quotation according to his command.
And on the same day, by his order, I wrote in the same
book no less than three other quotations pleasing to him,
as I had foretold.

Concerning the Contents of the Handbook.

And afterwards, day by day, in the course of the talk between us, as we kept our attention on this, other quotations,
just as pleasing, were found, and when that book was filled,
the volume grew, and rightly, as it is written, The just
builds on a small foundation, and little by little increases
it.   As the busy bee travels far and wide, searching
through the marshes, so without pause and unceasingly
did he gather many little flowers of Holy Scripture of
divers kinds, wherewith he filled full the cells of his
mind.

Now from the time of the writing of that first quotation, he straightway strove earnestly to read and to translate into the Saxon tongue, and after that to teach many
others.   And we may learn from that happy thief, who
knew the Lord Jesus Christ, his Lord, and, indeed, the
Lord of all, while he hung beside Him on the revered
gibbet, the Holy Cross.   For he addressed his prayers to
Him, bending on Him his bodily eyes, being able to do
nought else, as he was held quite fast by nails, and in
lowly voice cried to Him, with fervent prayers, " Christ,

remember me when thou comest into thy kingdom." And on the gallows he first began to learn the outlines of the Christian faith.

And this king, in the same manner, though he was placed in a different situation, being in the possession of royal power, by the inspiration of God, began to learn the outlines of the Holy Scripture on the sacred feast of Martin. And after that he learnt, so far as he might, the flowers which his masters had gathered on all sides, and he brought them all into the compass of a single book, though they were placed in no order, until that book became almost as large as a psalter. This book he used to call his Enchiridion, that is, his Handbook, because with the utmost care he kept it at his hand day and night, and in it he found, as he then said, no small solace.

CONCERNING THE SORROWS OF ALFRED.

But as was long since written by a certain wise man, Wakeful are the minds of those whose righteous care it is to rule. And I think that I must be very watchful since I have made some comparison, though by way of contrast, between that happy thief and the king. For a gibbet is hateful to every one, and everywhere it is accounted evil. But what is to be done, if one may not snatch himself away from thence, nor avoid it, nor by any means improve his case while he remains there? He must then, whether he will or not, endure his suffering with sorrow and sadness.

So that king was pierced with the many nails of tribulation, though he was placed in royal power. For from his twentieth year until his forty-fifth, in the which he now is, he was unceasingly wearied with the most heavy affliction of an unknown malady, so that he had no rest even for a single hour, in the which he did not either bear that ill or despair under fear of it, being almost overwhelmed with grief. Moreover he was troubled and with reason by the constant attacks of foreign peoples, which he bore constantly by land and sea, with no interval of rest. And what shall I say of his many wars against the pagans, and of his battles, and of the never-ending care of ruling his kingdom?

CONCERNING THE GLORY OF ALFRED.

Or what shall I say concerning the daily intercourse with the nations which dwell from the Tyrrhenian Sea unto the uttermost bounds of Ireland? For I have seen and read letters and gifts sent to him by Elias, patriarch of Jerusalem. What shall I say of the cities and towns which he restored, and of the others which he built, where before there had never been any? Or of the work in gold and silver, incomparably made under his direction? Or of the halls and royal chambers, wonderfully made of stone and wood by his command? Or of the royal residences, built of stone, moved from their former positions, and most beautifully set up in more fitting places by the king's command?

How the People Would not Help the King.

But, over and above that illness, he had much anxiety and many disputes with his own people, who would of their own free will help him with little or no labour for the general necessities of the realm. Yet, with the help of God, he alone held the rule of the kingdom, which he had once received. As a master pilot strives to bring his ship, filled with many riches, to the safe haven of his native land, where he would be, though nearly all his sailors are worn out, so the king permitted himself neither to faint nor to waver, though he was set amid the rough waves and various storms of this present life. His bishops and ealdormen and the most noble of the people, and his best-beloved thegns, and the reeves, to whom under God and the king all authority over the whole realm seems rightly to belong, he urged and bent most wisely to his will and to the common good of the whole kingdom, by constant and gentle teaching, by praising, by exhorting, by commanding, and in the end, after showing much patience, by heavy punishment of the disobedient, and by making their ignorant folly and obstinacy hateful in every way.

But despite his royal urging, his commands were not performed, owing to the slackness of the people, or work, begun late in time of need, was unfinished and resulted not in good for them who undertook it. I, therefore, can speak of fortresses, which he commanded and which have not been begun, or which, being begun too late, have not been brought to a perfect end, because the armies of the enemy broke in by land and sea, or because, as often happened, on every side, those who then opposed the commands of the king repented in vain and were ashamed when they were well-nigh desolate. For, by the witness of Scripture, I call repentance vain in which many men sorrow, who are stricken with heavy punishment for the many ill deeds that they have done.

But though, alas! alas! the fair-spoken may be terribly afflicted and moved to weeping at the loss of their fathers, their wives, their children and their servants, their slaves and their handmaidens, the labours of their hands and all their belongings, of what avail is that shameful repentance? For they can neither succour their relations who have been slain, nor deliver their captive ones from their hateful captivity, nor can they sometimes even help those of them who have escaped, since they have not wherewith to support their own life. Those who are grievously afflicted then repent when penitence is too late, and they mourn that they carelessly despised the commands of the king, and with all their voice do they praise the wisdom of the king, and they promise to perform with all their strength that which they before refused to do, that is, in the matter of building fortresses and in other things which are for the general good of the whole kingdom.

Concerning the Monastery of Athelney.

Here also I think that it would be wrong to pass over the vow of his most excellent contemplation and its result, which he was not able in any wise to put aside at any time, in good fortune or in ill. For while, as was his wont, he thought of the good of his soul, among other good works with which he was ever greatly occupied day and night, he commanded that two monasteries should be built.

One monastery was to be in the place that is called Athelney, which is on all sides surrounded by vast marshy tracts, which are impassable, and by waters: to which also none can approach in any way save by causeways or by one bridge, which has been built with skill and toil. It lay between two forts at either end, and on the western end of the bridge a very strong fort has been placed with very excellent labour by the command of the same king.

In this monastery he collected monks of divers races

and from every quarter, placing them together in the same. This he did because, at the first, he found none, noble or free man, who would of his own accord submit to the monastic life, except children, who by reason of their tender age were still unable in any wise to choose the good and to refuse the evil. For, indeed, since many years before that time the desire for the monastic life had utterly died away among all that nation, as it had done also among many others, and though very many monasteries have been built in that land, and still remain, yet none keep the rule of that life rightly. The reason I know not; perchance it is the result of the attacks of foreign races, which often make hostile incursions by land and sea; or, perchance, of the too great abundance of riches of every kind among that people; and I think that it was much more from the latter cause that the monastic life has become despised. For this reason he laboured to gather monks of different race in this monastery.

How John the Old Saxon was made Abbot of Athelney, and how the Monastery was filled with Monks.

And in the beginning he made John, a priest and monk, an old Saxon by race, abbot. Then he brought certain priests and deacons from across the sea, but with them he had not yet as many as he desired. He further gathered

very many of the same Gallic nation, and among them
were some children, whom he commanded to be brought
up in the same monastery, and at a later date to be raised
to the monastic order.   And in this same monastery I
saw one who was born of pagan race, and who was
brought up there, and who wore monastic dress, nor was
he the only one of that race.

How there was a plot in the Monastery against the Abbot.

Nor may I, by the reserve of dumb silence, commit to
oblivion a crime which was once perpetrated in that
monastery, though it was a foul crime.   For in all the
Scriptures the evil deeds of wicked men are recorded
together with the praiseworthy actions of the just, as tares
and darnel are sown among the crops of wheat.   Good
deeds are related that they may be praised and followed
and imitated, and that those who pursue them may be
held worthy of all honour and reverence.   But evil deeds
are recorded that they may be hated and reprobated and
in every way avoided, and that those who pursue them
may be chastened with all hatred and contempt and
punishment.

Now once, through the promptings of the devil, a
certain priest and a deacon, of Gallic race, of the number
of the same monks, were roused by some hidden envy.

And they were in secret so greatly moved against their abbot, the same John, that in the manner of the Jews they would have beset their lord with subtlety and have betrayed him. For they led away two young slaves of the same Gallic race by bribes, and wickedly instructed them to enter the open church armed at night, while all slept soundly in delightful peace of body. And they were to close this again after them in the usual way, and hidden in it to wait until the abbot came alone. And when, as his habit was, he should enter the church alone and privately, for the sake of prayer, and bending his knees to the earth before the holy altar, bowed himself, they should attack him and strive to slay him then and there. Then they should drag his dead body thence and cast it down before the door of a certain courtesan, as though he had been slain while in her company. So they plotted, adding crime to crime ; as it is said, The last error shall be worse than the first.

How the plot Failed of Success.

But, by the mercy of God, which is ever wont to help the guiltless, the evil plan of the wicked men was in great measure brought to nought, so that it did not altogether come to pass as they had intended.

Therefore all the evil learning was clearly explained by the evil teachers to the evil learners, and when the appointed night came, giving opportunity and promise of impunity, they shut the two young robbers, armed, in the church to await the coming of the abbot. Then at midnight John, as his habit was, secretly and unknown to any one, entered the church to pray, and with bended knees bowed himself before the altar. And those two robbers suddenly rushed on him with drawn swords and afflicted him with cruel wounds. But he, as was his wont, was ever swift in thought, and, as I have heard some tell of him, was not unskilled in warlike arts, had he not given all his mind to better study. So, as soon as he heard the sound of the robbers, and before he saw them, he fell fiercely upon them, ere he was wounded, and crying as loudly as he could, resisted them, shouting again and again that they were devils and not men. Nor did he know to the contrary, for he thought not that men would dare this deed. Yet was he wounded before his people came to his help.

Now his people were dumbfounded at this clamour, and especially when they heard the cry of " devils." And, terrified, and at their wits' end, they ran together from all sides to the doors of the church, and even those who were, in the manner of the Jews, betrayers of their Lord ran also. But ere they came the robbers fled with haste to the lairs near at hand in the marsh, leaving the abbot half dead. Then the monks surrounded their scarce breathing master, and with groaning and sorrow bore him home, while the guilty wept no less than the innocent.

Yet did not the mercy of God permit so great a crime to go unpunished. The robbers who had committed and all those who had incited to so great a wrong were caught and bound, and after many torments, died by a very evil death. And having thus related these things I return to the point whence I set out.

How the King Founded a Nunnery at Shaftesbury.

Moreover the same afore-mentioned king commanded a monastery for nuns to dwell in to be built without the east gate of Shaftesbury. In it he placed his own daughter Elgiva, a virgin dedicated to God, to be abbess. With her also many other noble nuns dwelt in the same monastery, serving God in the monastic life. These two monasteries he plentifully enriched with landed possessions and all wealth.

How Alfred was Devoted to the Service of God.

When these matters had been so settled, as was his habit, he thought within himself what he could yet add which would be more profitable to pious contemplation; and that which was begun not foolishly, was wisely found and more wisely observed. For he had heard that which was written of old time in the Law, that the Lord has promised to return His tithe many times over, and that this promise is faithfully observed, and that He will return his tithe many times over.

Then, moved by this example, and wishing to surpass the custom of his ancestors, this pious thinker promised that he would give the half of his service, both by day and night, to God, devotedly and faithfully, with whole-hearted zeal, over and above the half of all his wealth, which, being gained with moderation and justice, was wont to come to him year by year. And this, as far as human understanding could know and observe it, he strove with craft and wisdom to fulfil. But, as was his habit, he was careful to avoid that which Holy Scripture warns man against, saying, If thou offerest rightly, but dividest not rightly, thou dost sin. He considered how he might rightly divide that which he had freely devoted to God. And, as Solomon has said, the king's heart is in the hand of the Lord, that is, his counsel, so, being guided from on high, he commanded his officers to divide into two equal parts all the revenues of the taxes each year.

How he Provided for the King's Service.

And when the division had been so made, he assigned the first part to be devoted to secular matters, and this in turn he ordered to be divided into three parts.   And the first part under this division he distributed year by year to his warriors, and also to his noble thegns who were resident in turn in the royal court, performing duties and in many offices.

Now the royal household was always so managed in three relays.   The servants of the king were very wisely divided into three bands, so that the first band remained for one month in the king's court day and night performing its duties ; and when the month was ended and another band was come, the first went home, and there remained for two months, every one caring for his own needs.   And the second band, when the month was ended, and the third band was come, went home to remain there two months.   And this last band, when the service of one month was ended and the first band was come, went home and there remained two months.   And by this method of relays of this kind the work of service in the royal court was taken in turn all the days of this life.

How Alfred gave gifts to Craftsmen and to Strangers.

The first of these shares, then, did he distribute to such men, and to each according to his rank and according to his service.   But the second share he distributed to the craftsmen whom he had gathered from all nations, and whom he had with him in great numbers, who were men skilled in every earthly work.   And the third portion of the same he gave to the wayfaring men who came to him from every nation, lying near and far, and who sought from him wealth, and even to those who sought it not. To each he gave according to his rank in a manner worthy of praise and with marvellous system.   This he did gladly, as it is written, God loveth a cheerful giver.

How Alfred Devoted the half of his wealth to God.

But the second part of all his wealth, which came to him from every form of tax, and which were assigned to his treasury, with good-will he devoted to God, as we have already just stated, and he commanded his officers to divide it into four parts, in the following manner.

The first part under that division was to be very carefully distributed to the poor of every nation who came to him.   And in this he was mindful how much human understanding needs to take care that the opinion of the holy Pope Gregory be observed when, in his wise discussion of the division of alms, he says, "Give not little to him to whom much is due, or much to him to whom little is due; and give not nothing to him to whom something is due, or anything to him to whom nothing is due."

Then the second part he gave to the two monasteries,

which he had ordered to be formed, and to those serving
God in them, of which matters we talked at length a little
while ago.   The third part he gave to the school which
he had very carefully formed for many nobles of his own
people and also for boys of lower birth, and the fourth
part he distributed among the monasteries which were near
in all the land of the Saxons and in Mercia.   In some
years he either gave in turn to the churches and to the
servants of God dwelling in Britain and Cornwall, Gaul
and Armorica and Northumbria, and sometimes even in
Ireland, or intended to do so at a later day, if his life and
prosperity continued.

How Alfred Needed to Tell the Time.

When these things had been so settled in order by the
same king, being mindful of that passage in Holy Scripture, where it is said, Whosoever would give alms, must
first offer himself; he considered wisely what he might
offer to God of the service of his body and of his mind.
For he purposed to offer to God of this no less than of
his material wealth, vowing that with all his might, as far
as human weakness and his ability and means would permit, he would render to God, with a good heart, the fourth
part of the service of his body and of his mind, both by
day and by night.   But as owing to the darkness he could
in no wise discover the passing of the hours of the night,

and often on account of the thick rain and clouds could
not even tell the passing of the hours of the day, he began
to devise how by some fixed rule and with certainty he
might be able to keep this promise that he had vowed to
his life's end without faltering, while he trusted in the
mercy of God.

How Alfred Devised Means for Telling the Time.

And considering this with care for some while, at last
he found useful and wise counsel, and commanded his
chaplains to bring him wax in sufficiency. When it was
brought he ordered it to be weighed by pence in the
balance. And when as much wax had been measured as
was equal to seventy-two pence in weight, he ordered the
chaplains to make six candles, each as large as the other,
twelve inches being marked as the length of each. Then,
when this plan had been devised, those six candles burned
brightly for twenty-four hours day and night without fail-
ing, before the holy relics of the many chosen of God,
which he had ever with him in all places.

Sometimes, however, they could not burn and give light
for a whole day and night to the same hour as that at
which the candles had been lighted on the previous even-
ing. For the violence of the winds blew too much upon
them, since at times the wind blew day and night without

ceasing through the doors of the churches and the windows, and the chinks and holes in the woodwork, and the many rifts in the walls, and the thin tents. So the candles were made to burn too quickly and finished their course before the right hour. Wherefore he planned how he might prevent so great a draught of wind.

And having taken cunning and wise counsel, he ordered a lantern to be well made of wood and ox-horn, for the horns of oxen, when white and planed down to a thin sheet, are as clear as glass. So the lanterns were wonderfully made of wood and horn, as we have said above, and at night the candles placed in them, being hindered by no gusts of wind, gave as much light without as within, since he had ordered a door to be made of horn for the opening. And when this device had been so executed, six candles, one after another, burned for twenty-four hours without intermission, neither too quickly nor too slowly. And when they went out others were lighted.

How he Loved the Poor.

When all these matters had been so set in order it was his desire to preserve the half of his service, as he had vowed to God, and to increase it as much as he was able or had the means, or rather as far as human infirmity allowed. He was a careful searcher out of truth in judgments, and the more so owing to his care for the poor.

On their behalf, amid all the other duties of this present life, he was wonderfully solicitous day and night. And, indeed, in all that realm, the poor had no helpers, or but very few, save him alone, since almost all the great men and nobles of that land indeed had turned their minds to secular rather than to heavenly works. And each regarded rather his own temporal advantage than the good of all.

How Alfred Administered Justice, and how he Corrected his Judges.

And in judgment he sought earnestly the good of his people, gentle and simple. For they very often, at the meetings of the ealdormen and the reeves, disputed among them, so that hardly any of them would allow that the judgment of the ealdormen or reeves was right. And constantly driven by this obstinate disputing they were desirous to submit to the judgment of the king alone, and straightway hastened from every side to secure it. Yet he, who knew that there was some wrong on his side in a dispute, would not willingly go to the judgment of such a judge, though compelled to do so against his will in accordance with law and his promise. For he knew that there not one of his ill deeds could be concealed for a moment. Nor is that strange, since the king was a very skilled hunter in the execution of judgment as in all other things.

Now he carefully considered all the judgments of almost his whole realm, that had been given in his absence, as to what they were, whether just or unjust   And if he were able to discover any wrong in those judgments he would gently summon those judges to him of his own accord, and either in person or by some other faithful men would question them as to why they had judged so wrongly. He would inquire whether it was from ignorance, or from ill-will of any sort, from love or fear of any man, or from hatred of others, or from greed of any man's money. Then if those judges professed that they had so judged those causes for that they could come to no better understanding on the matter, he would correct their inexperience and foolishness with discretion and moderation.   And he would speak and say, "I marvel greatly at this your insolence, since by the gift of God, and by my gift, you have assumed the duties and rank of wise men, but have neglected the study and exercise of wisdom.   I command you, therefore, either to lay down here that exercise of earthly power which you enjoy, or to take care to apply yourselves with much greater zeal to the study of wisdom."

How the Judges Strove to Learn Letters, and Lamented their Lack of Learning.

And when they heard these words they were terrified and as if they had been corrected with the greatest judgment, the ealdormen and reeves strove to turn themselves with all their might to the work of learning justice. Wherefore in a marvellous way almost all the ealdormen, reeves and officers, who had been illiterate from infancy, studied the art of letters, preferring to learn an unwonted discipline with great toil than to lose the exercise of power.

But if any were unable to make advance in the liberal arts, either from age or from the too great slowness of an unaccustomed mind, he would command his son, if he had one, or some other, his near relative, or if he had no one else, even his own free man or his serf, whom he had long since urged to read, to read Saxon books to him day and night, whenever he should have any leisure. And sighing greatly from the bottom of their hearts, they mourned because in their youth they had not devoted themselves to such studies. And they deemed the youth of this age happy, since they were able to be happily learned in liberal arts, but they considered themselves wretched, since they had not in their youth learned letters nor were even able to do so in old age, though they ardently desired to do so.

Now we have set forth the zeal both of old and young in learning letters in order to increase knowledge of the same king.

NOTES

Page 1. *The Author's Prayer.* For the reason for calling this passage a prayer rather than a dedication, cp. Introduction, p. xxix.

Ibid. Ruler of all the Christians, etc. In this expression there is an obvious exaggeration, since it is not certain that Alfred had anything more than a merely nominal suzerainty over North Wales (cp. p. 61 and note), while the Christians of Northumbria were under Danish rule. In the kingdom of Guthrum another possible exception may be found (cp. note to p. 43). As the term "Britain" was frequently used in a restricted sense to exclude Scotland, the omission of the Scottish Christians hardly constitutes an additional exception. It may be added that "Britain" is used ambiguously in Asser, meaning sometimes Wales and sometimes England and Wales (cp. pp. 17, 11, etc.). Might it be that Asser here uses it in the former sense, and wishes to declare that only the Welsh who had submitted to Alfred were worthy of the name of Christians? It would be in accord with the purpose of the *Life* if the view contained in the Introduction be just (cp. Introduction, p. xxviii *et seq.*).

Ibid. Asser. For an account of Asser, cp. Introduction, p. xii *et seq.*

Ibid. Of the Angles and Saxons king. Cp. below, king of the Anglo-Saxons. It will be seen from the text (cp. pp. 6, 17) that Asser styles the predecessors of Alfred "kings of the West Saxons." Plummer (*Life and Times of Alfred*, p. 39) argues that the use of the term "Angul-Saxonum rex" is an indication of the enhanced position of the king. It may be added that it is in strict accord with the facts. Alfred had brought Western Mercia under his direct rule, and was therefore king of Angles as well as of Saxons. In the *Chronicle* he appears as "king of the West Saxons," but in the notice of his death we find that he "was king of all the Angle-kin, save that part of them which was under the rule of the Danes" (*Chronicle*, MS. A, *s. a.* 901). In his charters he appears as king of the "West Saxons," "Saxons," "Angles" and "Anglo-Saxons" (cp. Kemble, *Codex Dipl.* Nos. CCCIX, CCCXIV, CCCXVI, CCCXVIII and CCCXIX). But the authenticity of these charters is often very questionable, and it would be unsafe to argue from them as to the title which Alfred actually assumed : in his will (Kemble, No. CCCXIV) he is "king of the West Saxons." The title "king of the Anglo-Saxons" was used by Edward the Elder, but under Athelstan was abandoned in favour of the title "king of the Angles" (cp. Kemble, Nos. CCCXXXIV and CCCXLVIII, etc.).

Page 1. *Eight hundred and forty-nine.* As will be seen from the text the age assigned to Alfred does not always agree with this date for his birth. From 870 to 876 there is an error of one year, and for the rest of the work an error of three years. This is accounted for by the fact that under both 869 and 870 the king's age is given as twenty-one, while in 878 it is given as twenty-seven, no allowance being made for the omission of the annal for 877, and his age being repeated from the annal for 876 (cp. text). Under 853, he is said to have been in his eleventh year, in the MS. (according to Wise, who corrects the entry to "fifth" in his edition). Opinions differ as to the true date of Alfred's birth. Ramsay (*Foundations of England*, i. 247, note i) regards the entry "eleventh" under 853 as preserving the true date *i. e.* 843, on the ground that a journey to Rome at the age of four years is improbable, and that the change would make the story of the book more intelligible (cp. note to p. 19). Stubbs (Will. Malm., *Gesta Regum*, II, p. xlii) also rather inclines to accept this date, but points out the difficulty which at once arises as to the date of the *Life* (cp. Introduction, p. xxii). Plummer (*op. cit.*, pp. 67-70) points out that the best authority for the date of Alfred's birth is the genealogical table which occurs as a preface to MS. A of the *Chronicle*, and of which an older copy is printed by Sweet (*Oldest English Texts*, p. 179). Here Alfred is described as having passed his twenty-third year at the time of his accession, the date of which is given in the *Chronicle* as 871 : thus the date of his birth would be 848. It may be concluded that the true date is either 848 or 849 : the latter being the date given in the later chroniclers.

Page 1. *Wantage.* Wanating. Asser is the only authority for the birthplace of Alfred. But in support of the view that he is right, Pauli (*König Ælfred*, p. 63, note 2 ; p. 284 and notes) points out that Alfred remembered Wantage " in his later years with affection." It formed part of his gift in his will to his wife Elswitha (cp. Kemble, *op. cit.*, No. CCCXIV).

Ibid. Berkshire. Berrocscire.

Ibid. Wood of Berroc. The identification of this wood is quite uncertain.   Guest (*Or. Celticae*, ii. 152) says that it included Windsor forest.   It appears in a charter of John, in 1199, when it was granted to the nuns of Amesbury (*Monasticon*, ii. 336, No. III, ed. 1846).

Ibid. His genealogy. This genealogy is copied from that which appears in the *Chronicle*, MS. A, under 855. There is another genealogy which occurs as a preface to MS. A, and in other places (cp. Earle and Plummer, *Two Saxon Chronicles Parallel*, I, p. 1 ff., p. 66 ; II, p. 1 ff.).   Certain differences between the genealogy given in the text and that in the *Chronicle* are noticed below.

Ibid. Ethelwulf. King of the West Saxons, 839–856. (Cp. text, p. 5 *et seq.* and notes.)

Ibid. Egbert. King of the West Saxons, 802–839. He had been exiled under Beorhtric (cp. text, p. 11 *et seq.* and notes) but returned on his death and became king. He freed his kingdom from Mercian control, and established the supremacy of Wessex.

Ibid. Ealhmund. He was sub-king of Kent (*Chronicle*, MS. F, *s. a.* 784). A charter granted by him to Abbot Hwitred and the monastery of Reculver in 784 is printed in Birch (*Cart. Sax.*, No. 243), and in Kemble (*Cod. Dipl.*, No. MXIII). The grant was of the land of twelve ploughs at Sheldwick. But the genuineness of this charter may be doubted.

Ibid. Ingild. His death is mentioned in the *Chronicle*, s. a. 718.

Ibid. Ine. King of the West Saxons, 688–726. His fame depends mainly on his laws, which may be found in Thorpe (*Ancient Laws and Institutes*, II, p. 460 ff.).

Page 2. *Went to Rome.* The *Chronicle* (*s. a.* 855) says, " who afterwards went to Saint Peter and there afterwards ended his life."

The date of his abdication is placed by Bede (*Ecc. Hist.* V. 7 : ed. Plummer, I. 294) in 725 or 726 ; by the *Chronicle* in 728 (MS. A) or 726 (MSS. C, D, E). For the story of the way in which his wife, Ethelburga, persuaded him to go, see William of Malmesbury, *Gesta Regum* (ed. Stubbs, I. 35, note, and 39). He has been described as the founder of the Anglo-Saxon school at Rome, but there is no proof that he was (cp. note to p. 32).

Page 2. *Cuda.* His name should be more accurately Cutha. He is mentioned in the *Chronicle* as defeating Ethelbert of Kent (*s. a.* 568), and as fighting with the Britons (*s. a.* 571, MS. E, and *s. a.* 584, MSS. A and E). His death is given under 571 in MS. E, and under 584 in MSS. A and E.

Ibid. Cuthwin. He is mentioned in the *Chronicle* (*s. a.* 577) as sharing with Ceawlin in the defeat of the Britons at Deorham.

Ibid. Ceawlin. King of the West Saxons, 560–593. His reign was marked by the victory of Deorham, which divided the Welsh of Cornwall from those of Wales proper.

Ibid. Cynric. King of the West Saxons, 534–560.

Ibid. Creoda. His name is omitted in MS. A of the *Chronicle*, but occurs in MSS. B, C and D.

Ibid. Cerdic. Died in 534, according to the *Chronicle*. He is the traditional founder of the West Saxon kingdom. In the *Chronicle*, (*s. a.* 495) the arrival of the West Saxons is recorded as follows : "In this year came two ealdormen to Britain. Cerdic and Cynric his son, with five ships, came to the place that is called Cerdices-ora, and on the same day they fought with the Welsh."

Ibid. Elesa. In the *Chronicle* he is made the son of Esla, whose name Asser omits.

Ibid. Gewis. In the *Chronicle* the list reads, "Gewis was the son of Wig, who was the son of Freawin, who was the son of Frithogar." Asser omits these three names.

Ibid. Gegwis. Bede (*Ecc. Hist.*, III. 7) tells us that the West Saxons were called Gewissae in ancient times.

Ibid. Fingodwulf. Asser here coalesces two names, Fin and Godwulf, which occur in the *Chronicle* list.

Ibid. Sedulius. Coelius, or Gaius Coelius, Sedulius was a Christian poet who flourished about the middle of the fifth century. Beyond this approximate date nothing certain is known of him.

According to Isidore of Seville he was a priest : other writers have made him a bishop, but nothing definite can be asserted on this point. He seems to have died before 496, since his writings were collected after his death by Asterius, a consul, who is probably to be identified with Rufus Asterius, who was consul in that year. The chief poem of Sedulius is the *Carmen Paschale*, or *Mirabilium Divinorum Libri Quinque*. It is written in hexameters, and was possibly dedicated to Theodosius the Younger, which would place its date before 450. Sedulius also prepared a prose version of the *Carmen Paschale*, and wrote the following other poems : *Veteris et Novi Testamenti Collatio*, *Hymnus de Christo*, and *De Verbi Incarnatione*. (Cp. Smith, *Dict. of Greek and Roman Biography and Mythology*.) The works of Sedulius are edited by Hümer (in the *Corpus Scrip. Ecc. Lat.*, Vol. X).

Page 2. *In his Paschal Hymn*. The quotation is from the *Carmen Paschale*, i. ll. 17-26.

Ibid. Geta. Asser misunderstood the meaning of Sedulius, who was referring to the Geta who appears as a stock comic character in Terentian comedy (*e. g.* in the *Andria*).

Ibid. Caetwa. Taetwa in the *Chronicle*.

Page 3. *Hathra.* After his name the *Chronicle* (*s. a.* 855) adds, " who was born in the Ark." It then makes him the son of Noah (MS. A). MSS. B and C give Hwala and Bedwig as the text.

Ibid. Sem. Omitted in the *Chronicle*, MS. A. In MSS. B and C we have Sceaf, who is the subject of a legend which may be found in Ethelwerd (*M. H. B.*, p. 512B) and with some variations in William of Malmesbury (*Gesta Regum*, i. 121).

Ibid. Noe, etc. The genealogy as given in Luke iii. 36-38.

Ibid. Adam. After Adam the *Chronicle* adds, " the first man, and our Father, which is Christ. Amen." (MS. A, *s. a.* 855.)

Ibid. Osburh. Nothing is known of Osburh beyond the information contained in the text. She was the mother of Ethelbert, Ethelred and Ethelswith, as well as of Alfred, and possibly of Ethelbald also (but cp. note to p. 15). Athelstan, even if he were really the son and not rather the brother of Ethelwulf (cp. note to p. 5), can hardly have been the son of Osburh, since he was already of full age in 836. Ethelwulf married Judith in 855, and it has therefore been stated that Osburh died before that date. On the other hand, it has been suggested that she was divorced (by Freeman, *D. N. B.*, s. "Alfred"; Lappenberg, *Hist. of England*, trans. Thorpe, ii. 25, etc.), as this theory simplifies the story of the book (cp. p. 19 and notes), and also makes possible the alleged presence of Alfred's mother at Athelney (cp. notes to p. 37). The suggestion has been indignantly repudiated by Pauli (*op. cit.*, p. 61 ff), and Plummer (*op. cit.*, p. 84), who argue from the silence of authorities and the excellence of the character of Osburh; it is also pointed out that the difficulty in the story of the book does not really amount to much (cp. notes to p. 19). It may, however, be noted that Asser alone mentions Osburh: that he would hardly allude to the divorce of Alfred's mother in a book which Alfred might read, and that the character of Osburh is known only from the somewhat formal expressions in the text, and by deduction from the interest which she showed in Alfred's anxiety to possess the book. There is no particular reason for supposing that the character of Osburh was so remarkably fine, unless it be held that a good man must have had a good mother. A third explanation which would remove the difficulty of the book story, and of the Athelney story, and also the suggestion of stigma which a divorce might imply, may possibly be found in the parallel of Henry the Fowler. He contracted a marriage with Hathaburg, which was valid in Saxon law, but invalid in the eyes of the Church (cp. Thietmar, *Chronicle*, i. 5 (4)). From the text of Asser it would appear that there was some degree of consanguinity between Ethelwulf and Osburh, and it might be that the marriage was ecclesiastically invalid: such a marriage was perfectly honourable to both parties, but could easily be annulled for reasons of State, as was that of Henry the Fowler. Or again, as Ethelwulf was a very religious man, his conscience may have suddenly pricked him and led him to put away his wife. This explanation would assist in the explanation of the "anointing" of Alfred by the pope (cp. p. 6 and notes), since the sons of Osburh would be in the doubtful position which was occupied, *e. g.* by Thankmar (cp. notes, *loc. cit.*). It would also supply an additional motive for the rebellion of Ethelbald if he were not the son of Ethelwulf by Osburh. It may also be noted that while Ethelwulf caused Judith to be crowned, he did not do so in the case of Osburh (cp. p. 10 and notes).

Page 3. *Oslac.* Nothing else is known of Oslace. Kemble (*Saxons in England*, ii. 110–111) says that the office of butler was one of the great offices of State, a post " of the highest dignity and was held by nobles of the loftiest birth and greatest consideration." Stevenson (*Asser*, p. 164), however, rejects Kemble's view.

Ibid. Goths and Jutes. Stevenson (*op. cit.*, p. 166 ff) points out that Asser means to identify the Goths with the Jutes.

Ibid. Stuf and Wihtgar. In the *Chronicle* (*s. a.* 530, 534) we find an account of the acquisition of Wight, upon which the passage in the text is based : " In this year (530) Cerdic and Cynric took the Island of Wight and slew a few men at Wihtgaraesbyrg. 534. In this year Cerdic died, and Cynric, his son, succeeded him, and ruled from that time twenty-six winters : and they gave to their two nephews (*al.* cousins), Stuf and Wihtgar, the Island of Wight." Under the year 544, we find, " In this year Wihtgar died, and they buried him at Wihtgarabyrg." Plummer (*Earle and Plummer, op. cit.*, ii. 14) says that the entry under 544 proves that Wihtgar is a mere abstraction to account for the place name.

Ibid. Wihtgaraburh. Plummer (*ibid.*) points out that the name means the " burh of the Wight-dwellers." It has been identified with Carisbrook, but the identification is rejected by Stevenson (*op. cit.*, p. 172 ff).

Page 4. *How the men of Devon,* etc. This passage, and those which follow down to the end of the account of the victory of Athelstan, are drawn from the *Chronicle*, MS. E. In MS. A the order of events is different, being as follows : Victory of Ceorl ; victory of Athelstan ; the Danes winter ; burning of Canterbury and London ; defeat of Beortulf ; attack on Surrey ; battle of Aclea. In Ethelwerd (*M. H. B.*, 511, C. D.) the victory of Athelstan is placed first, and that of Ceorl is stated to have been seven years later. In the text, Asser adds the notes as to the situation of places for the benefit of his Welsh readers (cp. Introduction, pp. xxvii, xxx).

Ibid. Ceorl. A Ceorl witnesses a charter of Ethelwulf, Dec. 26, 847, granting himself land "in Hamme" (Birch, *Cart. Sax.*, No. 452). He appears as Ceorl " princeps," the latter being often an equivalent for "comes," ealdorman. For a discussion of the duties of the ealdormen and their number at this period, cp. Chadwick, *Studies on Anglo-Saxon Institutions* (pp. 166 ff).

Page 4. *Wicganbeorg.* This place has not been identified.

Ibid. Sheppey. In the *Chronicle* (MS. E, *s. a.* 851) the Danes are said to have wintered in Thanet : in MS. A the place at which they wintered is not given. Ethelwerd (511 D) gives Thanet as the place.

Ibid. A most excellent monastery. Minster in Sheppey.

Ibid. Dorubernia. Canterbury.

Ibid. London. Wise, in his edition of Asser, marks London as being interpolated here. But the sack of London is mentioned in the *Chronicle*, MS. A, though not in MS. E.

Ibid. Beortulf. King of the Mercians, 838 or 839 (?) to 852. Several alleged charters of this king are printed in Birch (*op. cit.*, Nos. 152, 428, 429, 430, 432, 433, 436, 454, 455 and 462). The charter of Beortulf to Croyland, given by Ingulf (ed. Birch, 20–25), is certainly a forgery.

Page 5. *Ethelbald.* Cp. *infra*, note to p. 15.

Ibid. Aclea. This place has not been identified. From Prudentius of Troyes (*s. a.* 850) we find that the Danish army was part of that of Rurik, which had divided.

Ibid. Athelstan. In the *Chronicle*, MS. A, *s. a.* 836, it is stated that Ethelwulf on his accession made his son Athelstan king over Kent, Essex, Sussex and Surrey. In MS. E, Athelstan is said to have been the son of Egbert. Ethelwerd (511 A, and 514 A) says that he was the eldest son of Ethelwulf ; the *St. Albans Chronicle* (Matt. Paris, *Chron. Maj.*, ed. Luard, I. 377) calls him an illegitimate son of Ethelwulf, but it may be suggested that this is a confusion due to the fact that the later Athelstan, son of Edward the Elder, is also said to have been illegitimate. It seems more probable that he was Ethelwulf's brother and that the subject of "selde" in MS. A is really Egbert (cp. Plummer, in *Earle and Plummer*, II. 75). As Ethelbert was made king of Kent in 855 (cp. note to p. 16), Athelstan must have died before that date. There is not the least ground for the identification of Athelstan with Saint Neot (cp. Pauli, *op. cit.*, 209–210).

Ibid. Nine ships. MSS. A and E agree in giving this number ; MSS. B and C say "eight." *Henry of Huntingaon* (ed. Arnold, p. 141) makes the victory of Athelstan a naval battle, but probably only because there is this reference to the capture of ships.

Page 5. *How Ethelwulf*, etc. This passage is drawn from the *Chronicle*. The reason for the appeal was the revival of Welsh power under Rhodri Mawr (Roderick the Great), 844–877.

Page 6. *Mid-Britons*. In the *Chronicle* the expression is North Welsh.

Ibid. Went into the land of the Britons. According to Caradoc (*Wynne*, ed. 1697, p. 27–28), Ethelwulf penetrated to Anglesey, " which he cruelly and miserably destroyed." On the same authority, the victory of the English was only a temporary one.

Ibid. How Alfred went first to Rome. In the *Chronicle* (*s. a.*) the following account is given of the first visit of Alfred to Rome : " And in this year did King Ethelwulf send his son Alfred to Rome. At that time the Lord Leo was pope at Rome, and he hallowed him to king and took him as his bishop's son." A letter of Leo to Ethelwulf is preserved, giving an account of the visit : " To Edelvulf, king of the English. We have well received your son, Erfred, whom you have at this time taken care to send to the shrines of the holy apostles, and as our spiritual son we have adorned him with the belt, dignity and garb of consular rank, in the manner of the Roman consuls, for that he delivered himself into our hands." This letter is printed by Stubbs (Will. Malm., *Gesta Regum*, II. xlii, note 4). Ethelwulf had long been considering a visit to Rome (cp. *infra*, note to p. 8).

Ibid. Leo. Leo IV, pope from 848 to 855

Ibid. Anointed him as king. This is obviously equivalent to the *Chronicle's* " to cyninge gehalgode," "hallowed to king." The passage has been explained in various ways. Stubbs (Will. Malm., *Gesta Regum*, II. xliii) says that the ceremony was that of confirmation, and was misunderstood by the Saxons. Lappenberg (*op. cit.*, II. 25) takes the passage literally, but cannot explain Ethelwulf's motive. Pauli (*op. cit.*, p. 68) suggests that Ethelwulf wished Alfred to succeed him. Plummer (*op. cit.*, p. 71) suggests that possibly Alfred was at this time given a titular sovereignty in Kent, or if this view cannot be admitted, he would regard the ceremony as being the investing of Alfred with consular rank, a view which is adopted by Stevenson (*op. cit.*, 179 ff), who adds that the ceremony amounted to little more than giving Alfred " a brevet of Roman nobility." To all these views there would appear to be objections. It seems rather a serious misunderstanding to take mere confirmation as being a hallowing to king, and the pope's letter (cp. above) would surely imply something more than a purely religious ceremony. Indeed, the phrase "took him to be his bishop's son" would appear to mean confirmation, in which case the "hallowed to king" must mean something more. Again, as Ethelwulf had three older sons, and as in his will he appears to have done what he could to secure the succession to the two eldest, it is hard to take the passage in its literal meaning. There is no evidence for Alfred holding any royal position in Kent : indeed, Ethelbert was afterwards definitely made king of that district (cp. note to p. 16). Finally there is no evidence that there was any anointing in connection with the elevation of a man to consular rank ; there is no evidence of the preservation of a special costume, such as might be confounded with royal robes ; and there is no evidence that the popes ever assumed at this period the right to confer such a dignity. The so-called "consulship" of Chlodwig, which might be quoted as giving evidence of a special costume was probably not a conferring of the consulship at all ; at least the case is a most doubtful one. And another possible exception, that of Charles Martel, to whom the consulship was offered, is probably not an exception at all. There is much reason for thinking that the pope was acting as the representative of the emperor, and with the emperor's direct sanction and command. It is, perhaps, by reference to parallel cases that the most probable explanation can be found. We find the very phrase which Asser here uses, "unxit in regem," used on the occasion of the anointing of the sons of Pippin by Pope Stephen (cp. *Vit. Stephani*, in *Lib. Pont.*, ed. Duchesne, I. 448 ; *Ann. Einhardi*, ed. Pertz, *s. a.* 753 ; etc.). In this case the anointing of the sons of Pippin was probably intended as the definite recognition of the father's newly acquired royal dignity ; it was, as it were, a declaration to the world in general, and to the Franks and Carloman in particular, that the house of Pippin was as truly royal as that of the Merovingians, and, moreover, that the claim of Pippin's sons to the succession was to be preferred to that of the sons of Carloman. It was intended to emphasise the "clausula" of Pope Zachary, which confined the succession to the direct heirs of Pippin (cp. Greg. Tours, *Opera*, in Migne : Pat. Lat., LXXI, 911). The position of Ethelwulf was in some respects not unlike that of Pippin. His father had secured the supremacy over the various Anglo-Saxon kingdoms for Wessex, but any guarantee that this supremacy would be permanent would be valuable. In the papal recognition of the fact that the son of Ethelwulf was of royal stock, such a guarantee might be found, at least the dignity of Ethelwulf's position would be enhanced. If there were any doubt as to the marriage with Osburh (cp. above note to p. 3) there would be an additional reason for securing recognition for Alfred, a reason which would appeal to so religious a man as Ethelwulf. According to this view the "anointed him as king" would mean "recognised him publicly as coming of royal stock." The expression in Asser may well be due to the influence of Frankish models (cp. Introduction, p. xxvi) ; and the phrase of the *Chronicle* either to a misunderstanding of the ceremony, or to the poverty of the Anglo-Saxon language.

Page 6. *How the Saxons fought the pagans,* etc. This passage is based on the *Chronicle,* s. a.

Page 7. *Ruim.* Guest (*Or. Celt.,* II. 153) says that this word means "foreland," and is preserved in Ramsgate.

Ibid. His daughter. Ethelswith. Her name occurs in the *Chronicle,* s. a. 888, where her death is recorded (cp. note to p. 32). Burhred succeeded Beortulf in 852.

Ibid. Chippenham. Asser adds the place of the wedding to the account in the *Chronicle.*

Ibid. How the pagans wintered in Sheppey. From the *Chronicle,* s. a. For the passage here interpolated, cp. *infra,* notes on the interpolations, p. 146.

Page 8. *How Ethelwulf gave gifts,* etc. This passage is based on the *Chronicle,* s. a. Asser supplies the information that Alfred went with Ethelwulf to Rome.

Ibid. The tenth part of his whole realm. In the *Chronicle* the grant of Ethelwulf is recorded in the following terms : "And in this year did King Ethelwulf convey by a charter the tenth part of his land throughout his realm to the glory of God and to his own everlasting salvation." Pauli (*op. cit.,* p. 71–72, and note 3) says that this must mean the tenth part of his private possessions. Kemble (*op. cit.,* II. 481–490) says that there were two grants, one on this occasion and one at his death. He adds that as Ethelwulf can have had no territory, this must mean that he gave up his royal rights over a tenth of the realm, and he concludes that there were three grants in all. The first released a tenth of all the land from everything except the three necessary duties ; the second gave one-tenth of his private estates to thegns or clerks ; the third provided for the entertainment of a poor man on every ten hides of land.

Page 8. *He went to Rome.* Ethelwulf had long been meditating a journey to Rome, and as early as 839 he applied to Lewis the Pious for a safe conduct (Prud. Troyes, *s. a.*). On this occasion he urged Lewis to pay attention to the salvation of the souls of his subjects, explaining that a vision had appeared to one of his subjects warning him of the evils which would shortly come upon the world if there were not a reformation of manners. Prudentius (*loc. cit.*) gives us the details of the vision. The zeal of Ethelwulf with regard to his visit to Rome, and for religious matters generally, may be the origin of the story that he was educated for the church, which occurs in William of Malmesbury (*Gest. Pont.*, ed. Hamilton : 160–161). In *Henry of Huntingdon* (p. 141–142) he is declared to have been bishop of Winchester at the time of Egbert's death, but "driven by force of circumstances, he became king, married, and begat four sons, who were all kings after his day." This is an interesting example of the growth of a legend ; it may be paralleled, perhaps, in the story that Henry VIII was designed for the archbishopric of Canterbury. Ethelwulf seems to have maintained close relations with the continent. In the letters of Lupus of Ferrières (Migne, Pat. Lat., Vol. 119, col. 451 *et seq.*) we find a letter (No. XIII) to the king congratulating him on his piety ; and from the same source (Letter XIV) we learn that Ethelwulf had a Frankish secretary or messenger, called Felix. On his arrival in the Frankish kingdom, Ethelwulf was entertained by Charles the Bald, who conducted him as far as the frontiers of his realm (Prud. *s. a.* 855). In the course of the journey he visited Lupus (cp. Letter XLIII).

Ibid. There he remained one full year. In the *Life* of Benedict III (*Lib. Pont.*, ed. Duchesne, II. 148) there is an account of Ethelwulf's visit and of the gifts which he made to the churches and to the pope. The author of the *Life* failed to gather the king's name.

Ibid. Judith. Daughter of Charles the Bald, king of the West

Franks, 840–877, and emperor, 875–877. She was twelve years of age at the time of her marriage to Ethelwulf. She was betrothed to him in July and married in October 15 (Prud. *s. a.* 856), at Verberie, near Senlis, by Hincmar, archbishop of Rheims. The marriage service is preserved in *Bouquet* (VII. 621), and consisted of the invocation of blessings on the queen, the actual marriage, a prayer for the preservation of her chastity, the coronation, and a final blessing. Lappenberg (*op. cit.*, II. 26–27) suggests that the idea of the marriage was to improve the relations between Wessex and the continent ; it may be added that any measure which was calculated to render the journey of the English pilgrims to Rome more secure would necessarily appeal to a man of Ethelwulf's religious character.

Page 8. *How Ethelbald*, etc. There is no other authority for the conspiracy of Ethelbald, though the *Liber Pontificalis* (*loc. cit.*), may hint at it when it says that Ethelwulf "left all his possessions and lost his own realm." The expression may, however, equally be mere exaggeration. The St. Albans chronicler (Matt. Paris, ed. Luard, *Chron. Maj.*, I. 385) says that the cause of the revolt was twofold. In the first place the coronation of Alfred, which seemed to exclude the other sons from the succession (and which the chronicler places on the occasion of Ethelwulf's visit to Rome), and in the second place the marriage of Ethelwulf with Judith, which seemed to indicate contempt for the women of England, combined to alienate Ethelbald and his friends. An additional cause was supplied by the fact that it was reported in England that Judith had been called "queen" and placed beside her husband at meat, by command of that husband. Lappenberg (*op. cit.*, II. 27) accepts this idea as to the causes of the rebellion. Pauli (*op. cit.*, p. 75–76) suggests that Ethelbald had been regent during his father's absence and was reluctant to part with his authority. The view is supported by the fact that the *Chronicle* (*s. a.* 855), in mentioning the accession of Ethelbald, gives him five years as the length of his reign, while it also (*ibid.*) states that Ethelwulf died two years after his return from Rome in 855, and that Ethelbald died in 860 (*Chronicle*, s. a.). Pauli adds that Ethelbald possibly considered that his father was too weak to cope with the dangers which threatened Wessex, and that he may have remembered the troubles which followed the marriage of Lewis the Pious to Judith's grandmother and namesake. It seems true in any case that on the eve of his departure to Rome Ethelwulf had divided his kingdom on the same principles on which it was divided at his death (cp. *infra*, p. 16 and notes). It is quite possible that the object of Ethelbald was merely to keep that of which he was already in possession; in which case he was successful. Plummer (*op. cit.*, 78–79) regards the story as being untrue; he points out the remark of the *Chronicle* on the subject of Ethelwulf's return, "and his people were fain of him." But it may be pointed out that the phrase used is identical with that used on the occasion of the emerging of Alfred from Athelney, and therefore the expression might be taken to hint at trouble in his absence. A further argument in favour of the view that there actually was such a conspiracy may be found, perhaps, in the character of Ethelbald (cp. *infra*, note to p. 15).

Page 8. *Ealhstan.* Cp. *infra*, note to p. 22 for the character of this bishop.

Ibid. Eanwulf. He is mentioned in the *Chronicle* (*s. a.* 845) as defeating the Danes at the mouth of the Parret. In 854 he occurs as witness to a charter of Ethelwulf (Birch, No. 474).

Page 9. *That king was froward*, etc. This is Ethelbald, and the allusion is, no doubt, to the acts which are recorded of him after his father's death (cp. p. 15 and notes). As will appear, the character of Ethelbald was quite unlike those of his brothers (cp. notes to p. 15).

Ibid. How Ethelwulf returned, etc. His return, and the cordial reception which he received from his subjects, are recorded in the *Chronicle* (*s. a.* 855), where we read, "and after that he returned to his people, and they were fain of him."

Ibid. The kingdom . . . was divided. This story of the division of the kingdom has been made the ground for an attack on the authenticity of this passage, but, as is pointed out by Stevenson (*op. cit.*, p. cxxi), such divisions were not uncommon in the continental history of this period.

Ibid. Eastern districts. Page 10. *Western Districts.* Ethelwulf retained Kent, Sussex, Surrey and Essex; Wessex went to Ethelbald cp. *infra*, p. 16 and note). It may, perhaps, be suggested that this division was that which the older king would naturally have desired; he was left that part of England which was the more important ecclesiastically. On the other hand, Ethelbald secured at least his ancestral inheritance, if the expression may be permitted, without the possibility of being excluded from the throne by his father's partiality for his youngest son. It is perhaps interesting to note that Asser says that the west has always been more important than the east part of the kingdom. It was certainly true that Wessex was the backbone of the " English " kingdom, but Asser, as an ecclesiastic, might have almost been expected to forget this and to assign the superiority in importance to the seat of the archbishopric. That he does not do so may possibly supply additional internal evidence of the Welsh origin of the *Life of Alfred*.

Page 10. *How King Ethelwulf*, etc. She had been already crowned, on the occasion of her marriage (cp. *supra*, note to p. 8.) The previous denial of the title of queen is mentioned in Prudentius (*s. a.* 856).

Page 11. *The story of Queen Eadburh*. This story is known only through Asser. The marriage of Eadburh to Beorhtric is mentioned in the *Chronicle* (*s. a.* 787), " King Beorhtric took Eadburh, daughter of Offa, to wife." Under 836, in mentioning the death of Egbert, the *Chronicle*, MS. A, supplies us with additional information : " In this year did King Egbert die, and him Offa, king of the Mercians, previously, and Beorhtric, king of the West Saxons, had driven him for three years from the land of the Angle-kin to Frankland, before that he became king, and Beorhtric aided Offa, because he had his daughter to his queen." The literal rendering of the *Chronicle* rather seems to misrepresent the actual cause of events. Beorhtric persuaded Offa to exile Egbert undoubtedly. William of Malmesbury (*Gesta Regum*, I. 43 : cp. I. 91, I. 105) explains that the result of the marriage was the expulsion of Egbert from Mercia, and implies that it was to procure this expulsion that the marriage was concluded by Beorhtric. This is no doubt a legitimate deduction from the words of the *Chronicle*. The whole story of Eadburh receives some confirmation, as will be seen below, and there is no reason for regarding it as altogether untrue. On the other hand, Asser may have " edited " the account as he received it from Alfred.

Ibid. My truth-telling lord. Apparently the only other occasion on which this epithet is applied to Alfred is in Hermannus, *De Miraculis Sancti Eadmundi* (*Mem. of Saint Edmund's Abbey*, ed. Arnold, I. 29), " his brother and successor, Alfred the truth teller."

Page 11. *Teutonic nations.* Theotisci. For a note on the origin and use of this term for the German races, cp. Stevenson (*op. cit.,* p. 202 *et seq.*).

Ibid. From my truth-telling lord. The fact that Asser quotes Alfred as his authority has been made the basis of an attack on the genuineness of the work, since it was alleged that the story would be generally well known. But as Stevenson points out (*op. cit.,* p. ci), there is no reason to believe that the details of the story would be so very generally known. It may be added that when it is remembered that the work was intended not for English but for Welsh readers (cp. Introduction, p. xxvii) the objection falls to the ground entirely.

Ibid. Offa. King of Mercia, 755–794. Under him the power of Mercia perhaps reached its greatest height, and Offa is well known as the correspondent of Charles the Great. He went on a pilgrimage to Rome, and is said, though without proof, to have founded the Anglo-Saxon School there, and to have instituted Peter's Pence for its support. According to another account he restored it (cp. *supra,* note to p. 2, and *infra,* note to p. 32).

Ibid. A great dyke. Offa's dyke, of which considerable traces still remain, ran from the mouth of the Dee to that of the Severn ; it consisted of an embankment and a ditch. It has been suggested that Offa merely repaired a previous work, which had already served as the frontier between Mercia and the Welsh. On the other hand, it has been regarded as the result of the " devastation of the southern Britons" mentioned in the *Annales Cambriae* (*s. a.* 778, 784), and as indicating the extension of the Mercian frontier from the Severn to the Wye (cp. Hodgkin, *Pol. Hist. of England,* p. 251).

Ibid. Beorhtric. King of the West Saxons. He succeeded the murdered Cynewulf in 784 (*Chronicle,* s. a. ; cp. *s. a.* 755), but was not the son of that king. It would appear that he usurped the throne, if the throne be regarded as hereditary, at the expense of Ealhmund, Egbert's father.

Page 12. *A certain young man.* In the *Chronicle,* MS. A (*s. a.* 802), we find the entry, " In this year King Beorhtric died, and Worr the ealdorman." It has been suggested that this is a tacit reference to the crime of Eadburh, and the Worr of the *Chronicle* is the " certain young man " of the text. In a charter of Beorhtric (Birch, No.

CCLXXXII) we find among the witnesses, "Wor princeps." In this same charter we find Eadburh sharing with her husband in a grant of land, but of course the authenticity of the charter is open to dispute.

Page 12. *My son.* Charles had asked Offa for the hand of one of his daughters for his son, Charles (*Gesta Abb. Font.*, p. 5), and it is possible that the daughter in question was Eadburh. As the younger Charles was alive in 802, and was never married, it is also possible that he is the son of the story. It has been suggested that Charles had some idea of influencing Wessex by a marriage between his son and the ex-queen ; but it is hard to see how influence could have been acquired in this way, even if the marriage had taken place.

Page 13. *A great monastery of nuns.* There is no clue at all to the situation of this monastery, and the remainder of the story rests on the authority of Asser alone, without even indirect support.

Ibid. Concerning the will of King Ethelwulf. The will of Ethelwulf has not been preserved, though the provisions contained in it as to the private inheritance of the king are recorded in Alfred's will (Birch, No. CCCXIV ; a Latin version in Camden ; *Anglica, Normannica, etc.*, p. 22). The account given by Alfred is as follows : "I, King Alfred, by God's grace and with the approval of Archbishop Ethelred, and the testimony of all the council of the West Saxons, have taken thought concerning the needs of my soul and concerning my property, which God and my parents gave to me, and concerning the heritage which King Ethelwulf, my father, bequeathed to us three brothers, Ethelbald and Ethelred and me, on condition that whichever of us should live the longest should receive it all. And it happened that Ethelbald passed away, and we two, Ethelred and I, with the witness of all the council of the West Saxons, transferred our part to King Ethelbert, our relative, on condition that he should again hand it over to us as it was when we entrusted it to him. And so did he, handing over both the inherited property and that which he accumulated among our people, and that which he himself acquired. And when it happened that Ethelred succeeded, then before all our counsellors I made request to him that we should divide the inheritance, and that he should give me my share. Then he said to me that he could not easily divide it, because he had tried to do so often before, and he said that what he should enjoy and

acquire in our nation he would, after his death, give to no one but
me, and then was I well satisfied at that. But it chanced that we
were all harassed by the heathen. Then we two spake of our
children that they required something to be done for them whatever
might befall us in these troubles. We were then at a meeting at
Swinburh, and then we said, in the presence of the council of West
Saxons, that whichever of us should survive should give the children
of the other those lands which either of us should have acquired, and
those lands which King Ethelwulf gave to either of us in the lifetime
of Ethelbald, with the exception of that which he bequeathed to us
three brothers. And each of us gave the other his pledge for this,
that whichever of us lived the longer he should take both the land
and the treasures and all his possession except that which each of
us bequeathed to his children. And it happened that King Ethelred
passed away. Then no man told me of any will or of any testimony
that it should be any other than as we two had formerly agreed in
the presence of witnesses. Then we heard of much contention as
to the succession, and thereupon I brought King Ethelwulf's will
before our council at Langenden, and it was read before all the
council of the West Saxons. When it had been read I asked them all
out of love to me, offering my pledge that I should never reproach any
of them because they should have spoken right, and besought them
that none of them should hesitate from love or fear of me to pro-
nounce judgment in the case, that none might say that I judged
unjustly the children of my kin, either older or younger. And then
they all pronounced right, and said that they could not think of any
juster law nor hear of any in the will. 'Now it is all handed over
to thy hand, and thou mayest bequeath and transfer it to relative or
stranger, whichever thou dost prefer.' And they gave their testimony that in this life none should ever turn it in any other way
except as I might myself bequeath it at my last day." (Translation
from the text in Birch, *loc. cit.*) It has been held by Lappenberg
(*op. cit.*, II. 27) and Pauli (*op. cit.*, p. 79) that Ethelwulf meant to
divide his kingdom and to found a distinct succession in Kent, and
that this is what is implied in the will. On the other hand, Plummer
(*op. cit.*, p. 86) does not admit this theory. It would seem to be
clear that in the will as represented in that of Alfred there is no
reference to anything but the private property of the king, while on

the other hand it is clear from the *Chronicle* (*s. a.* 855) that whether in accordance with the wish of Ethelwulf or no, the kingdom was for a time divided on his death (cp. p. 16). It must be remembered that the union of Wessex and Kent, using the latter term in its wider significance to include Surrey, Sussex and Essex, was of very recent date. We have already seen that under Beorhtric, Ealhmund was king of Kent (*supra*, note to p. 1), and that under Ethelwulf himself, Athelstan was in a similar position (cp. *supra*, p. 5 and note). The tendency was certainly centrifugal, and it may well have been out of the power of Ethelwulf to resist it. It may be that, recognising the impossibility of maintaining complete unity, he tried to limit the extent of the disruption by providing for the disposal of his private property in such a way as to emphasise the unity of his family. On the death of Ethelbald, the self-denial of Ethelred and Alfred, or the danger from the Danes, secured the succession of Ethelbert to the whole kingdom. And in order to avoid disputes as to the royal inheritance, the reigning king was given a life interest in the whole.

Page 14. *The money that he left behind him should be justly divided.* Cp. above, note to pp. 8 and 13.

Ibid. Three hundred mancuses. A mancus was one-eighth of a pound : thirty pence (cp. Hodgkin, *op. cit.*, p. 232 *et seq.*). Nothing is otherwise known of the bequests of Ethelwulf for charitable or religious purposes at Rome ; the assertion of William of Malmesbury that he instituted "Rome-scot" or "Peter's pence" (cp. Will. Malm., *Gesta Regum*, I. 109) is not supported by any earlier evidence.

Page 15. *How Ethelbald ruled the West Saxons.* The accession of Ethelbald is thus described in the *Chronicle*, MS. A, *s. a.* 855 : "Then the two sons of Ethelwulf began to reign ; Ethelbald began to reign in Wessex, and Ethelbert to reign in Kent, and to reign in Essex, and to reign in Surrey and Sussex." MSS. E and C omit Essex, and Asser does this also in describing the reunion of the two parts of the kingdom (cp. p. 16 and note).

Ibid. The prohibition of God. The allusion is more especially to 1 Cor. v. 1, which is practically paraphrased in the text.

Ibid. Married Judith. The marriage of Ethelbald to Judith is known only through Asser and the Frankish chronicler, Prudentius, who (*s. a.* 858) says, "Edilvulf" (Ethelwulf) "king of the West Saxons, died ; and Adalbold" (Ethelbald), "his son, married his widow, Queen Judith." Hincmar (cp. *infra*) implies the marriage. The *St. Albans Chronicle* (Matt. Paris, *Chron. Maj.*, I. 387) states that Ethelbald subsequently repented of his error and put away Judith ; and according to Rudborne (Wharton, *Ang. Sacra*, I. 204) he did this on the representation of Swithun. But these accounts look rather like the ordinary mediæval additions to genuine stories, which generally give a delightfully moral ending to such narratives : and that of Rudborne, in particular, seems like an attempt to make Saint Swithun do his duty. There is no evidence for such a divorce in any contemporary ; on the contrary, Hincmar (cp. *infra*) definitely styles her "the widow of Ethelbald." It is, indeed, somewhat remarkable that the marriage should not have created any sensation on the continent, and that Hincmar should have regarded it as lawful, since he was strongly opposed to Lothar II for repudiating his wife and marrying Waldrada (cp. Hincmar, *Ann.*, s. a. 862 *et seq.*). On the death of Ethelbald Judith returned to the continent, and her subsequent history is thus related by Hincmar (*Ann.*, s. a. 862 and 863). On her return to the continent she resided for a time at Senlis, under the care of the archbishop ; but presently eloped with Baldwin, count of Flanders, in disguise and with the assent of her brother, Lewis. Charles the Bald secured her excommunication, and that of her accomplices, in accordance with the decretals of Gregory the Great, from a council of bishops and nobles. Baldwin and Judith were supported by Lothar II, probably owing to the fact that he also had matrimonial difficulties. Eventually Charles was reconciled with his daughter at the request of the pope, and allowed her to be married to Baldwin. In the letters of Pope Nicholas I (*Bouquet*, VII, pp. 387 *et seq.* : Letters V, X, XIV ; Migne, Pat. Lat., Vol. 119, Letters XXII, XXIII, XXXVI) we find reference to the subject of the elopement of Judith with Baldwin, and there is also a letter of Hincmar on the subject (Migne, Pat. Lat., Vol. 126, col. 25–46 ; Vol. 135, Flodoard, *Hist. Ecc. Rem.*, III. xii). It may be noted that Flodoard (*loc. cit.*) makes Ethelwulf and Ethelbald identical, and Plummer (*Earle and Plummer*, op. cit., II. 81) suggests that this is an effort to " cover up the scandal." On the other hand, Hincmar, as already stated, does not appear to be aware that the scandal existed, and it seems more probable that Flodoard confused the two names. At a later date Johannes Longus sneers at the English for their ignorance of Christian doctrine, on the ground that they felt no concern at Ethelbald's action (Pertz, *Mon. Ger.*, xxv. 768 : quoted by Plummer, *Earle and Plummer*, op. cit., loc. cit.). By her marriage with Baldwin she became the ancestress of Matilda, wife of William I. She had three children by Baldwin : Baldwin II, count of Flanders, who was surnamed the Bald, in compliment to his maternal grandfather ; Raoul ; and Winidilda, who married Wifred, count of Barcelona (*l'Art de vérifier les dates*, XIII. 281–282).

Page 15. *Two years and a half.* For the possible explanation of the variation between the duration of Ethelbald's reign here given, and that in the *Chronicle* (cp. *supra*, note to p. 8).

Ibid. He raged and ruled. In *Henry of Huntingdon* (ed. Arnold, p. 142) we have a very different account of the reign of Ethelbald : " the most noble king " (*sc.* Ethelwulf) " at his death left his hereditary kingdom to Ethelbald, his son ; to his other son, Ethelbert, he left Kent, Essex and Sussex. These two brothers, being young men of excellent character, ruled the kingdom in great happiness while they both lived. And when Ethelbald had held his kingdom for five years, in peace, he was caught away by an untimely death, but all England lamented the youthful king, and great was the lamentation made over him. And they buried him at Sherborne. Then did England know how much she had lost in him." An account of the subsequent disasters follows. Plummer (*op. cit.*, pp. 86–87) regards the remarks both of Asser and of Henry of Huntingdon on the character of Ethelbald's reign as " mere rhetorical flourishes." On the other hand, there is a certain amount of evidence in favour of the view that Ethelbald was a man of violent but able character. All that Asser has to say of him supports the idea of his " frowardness," while the fact that his reign is a blank in the *Chronicle* would seem to prove that Wessex was free at this time from Danish attacks. There would seem indeed to be a marked contrast between the character of Ethelbald and that of his father and brothers. We have evidence of the piety of Ethelwulf (cp. p. 14), of the gentleness of Ethelbert (cp. p. 16 and *Chronicle*, s. a. 860), of the attention given by Ethelred to religious observances (cp. p. 26) : and there is no doubt of the sincere Christianity of Alfred. On the other hand, in Ethelbald we have a man who was sufficiently devoid of religious scruples to marry his step-mother, and who had already rebelled against his father. As already suggested, there is a temptation to account for the difference in character by supposing that Ethelbald was not the son of Osburh, an explanation which would also account for his rebellion in some measure (cp. *supra*, note to p. 8). It may be objected that in Alfred's will there is no hint that Ethelbald was not his full brother (cp. *supra*, note to p. 13, for the text of the will).

Page 15. *How Edmund*, etc. For a note on this interpolation, cp. *infra*, notes on the interpolated passages, p. 147.

Page 16. *Ethelbert . . . added Kent*, etc. Asser has put the facts in the reverse order. In the *Chronicle* (*s. a.* 855) it is mentioned that on the death of Ethelwulf, Ethelbert began to reign over Kent, Surrey, Sussex and Essex : and (*s. a.* 860) that on the death of Ethelbald the kingdom was reunited under Ethelbert. Therefore Ethelbert did not add Kent to his dominions, but added Wessex. As compared with the *Chronicle*, Asser omits Essex, and it has been suggested by Pauli (*op. cit.*, p. 81, note 4) that the explanation of this consists in the fact that Essex was already in the power of the Danes.

Ibid. Attacked . . . Winchester and sacked it. These events are recorded in the *Chronicle* (*s. a.*), from which Asser takes his account. From Hincmar (*Ann.*, s. a. 861) it would seem that the leader of the Danes in this attack was Weland. Further details as to Weland's career are to be found in Hincmar (*s. a.* 862) : he became a Christian and submitted to Charles the Bald.

Ibid. Five years . . . reigned Ethelbert. Henry of Huntingdon (p. 142) says that Ethelbert reigned five years in Wessex, ten in Kent. He certainly believed that Ethelwulf had provisionally divided his kingdom on the eve of his departure for Rome.

Page 17. *How the pagans*, etc. This passage is based on the *Chronicle*, s. a. 865.

Ibid. Eight hundred and sixty-four. The date in the *Chronicle* is 865, and the error is probably due to a transcriber.

Ibid. The men of Kent promised . . . money. Ethelwerd (512 D) relates these events, and adds, " and on their side they (*sc.* the men of

Kent) made ready money, being ignorant of that which should follow." He clearly laments the useless attempts to buy off the invader. It may be noted that this passage disposes of the popular idea that it was Ethelred II who first tried to buy off the Danes.

Page 17. *How Ethelred*, etc. This passage is based on the *Chronicle*, s. a. 866.

Ibid. Danubia. Denmark, according to Plummer (*op. cit.*, p. 41), who suggests that in Asser "Germania" means Norway, and "Danubia" Denmark. Stevenson (*op. cit.*, p. 217), on the other hand, regards the use of this word as showing that Asser somehow connected the Danes and the Danube, unless the word is due to the error of a scribe. The Danes, he points out, actually came from the mouth of the Rhine. The idea of a scribal error seems most probable. There is another explanation of the use of the term Germania, upon which Plummer relies for his argument (cp. p. 48 and note). In the *Chronicle* there is no mention of the place from which this Danish army came.

Page 18. *What little has come to my knowledge.* This is the first of the two places in which Asser mentions the proposed contents of his work : it will be seen that he does not define his object (cp. Int., p. xxviii *et seq.*).

Ibid. United and ardent love of his father and mother. It will be seen that this refers to his infancy and boyhood. The latter term is somewhat indefinite, but if Osburh died in or before 855, when Alfred was seven years old, it is hard to see how she could have cherished him greatly during his boyhood, since between one and two of the seven years of his life had been spent at Rome.

Ibid. Culpable negligence of his relations. "Parentes" is the word in the text, which does not necessarily mean "parents" (cp. Du Cagne, *sub. verb*). As the "united and ardent" care of his parents has just been mentioned, "relations" appears to be the only rendering of the word which is not in flat contradiction with the context. Pauli (*op. cit.*, p. 66) makes the passage refer to Judith, but it is surely rather unfair to accuse her of neglecting Alfred's education when she herself was only a mere child. On the score of his supposition that Ethelwulf was a learned king, Wright made this passage an additional ground for an attack on the genuineness of Asser, but Stevenson (*op. cit.*, p. c.) has shown that there is no real ground for the attack. As to the "nutritores," those who had care of him, this may mean merely those who had charge of him on his visits to the continent : the only occasions when he would be parted from his "relatives."

Page 19. *How Alfred obtained a book*. There are two main difficulties as to this passage. The first is as to the identity of the mother, but she cannot be Judith for the same reason as it is unfair to accuse Judith of having been guilty of culpable negligence in respect of the education of Alfred (cp. *supra*, note to p. 18) : she was only about seventeen when she returned to the continent. The second difficulty is as to the date of the incident. If Osburh were the mother, and it would appear that she must be, and if she died in 854–855, this would place the book incident not later than his sixth year : *i. e.* just before his second visit to Rome where he remained one year. To this there are two objections. If he learnt to read at so early an age, the neglect of his education was not very serious. It may be answered that the passage does not involve the supposition that he learnt to read, but merely that he repeated the contents of the book from memory. Plummer (*op. cit.*, p. 83, and note 3) rejects this solution on the ground that "recitare" is "to read aloud," and not to "repeat." But it means "repeat" both in classical and in mediæval Latin (cp. Mar. 9, 83 ; Du Cagne, *sub. verb* ; *Vulgate*, Tobit iii. 25). It is true that on the other occasions when it is used in Asser it means "read aloud" in most instances certainly, and perhaps in all. But on one occasion, in the account of the origin of the Handbook, it would seem quite as likely to mean " quote," while on another occasion (in the description of Alfred's energetic pursuit of letters) it might bear that meaning (cp. p. 69 and p. 63). Again, the fact that the word "legit" is used—"he went to his master and read it"—is not conclusive against this meaning for " recitare " : rather it might be taken to mean that he " read " the book with a master, and then "repeated" it. In this connection, the fact that Asser introduces the book story with an " ergo " may be of interest ; if we omit the intervening clause as to his skill in hunting, the conjunction becomes quite natural. He was ignorant of letters, but could memorise with ease, *therefore* it occurred to his mother to encourage his taste in this respect by showing him the book. The second difficulty arises from the expression that he was "ignorant of letters until his twelfth year." This must mean that he could not read. Later on (*infra*, p. 69) we are told that he began to read and to translate Latin after 884, *i. e.* not until his thirty-sixth or thirty-seventh year at earliest. The statement here therefore cannot mean merely that he was unable to read Latin, but that—as we should put it—he did not know his A B C. Ignorance of Latin, despite the fact that most books were in Latin, could hardly be regarded as the result of culpable negligence ; and later we find that he could read Saxon books (if "recitare" means "to read") before he could read Latin (cp. *infra*, p. 54). According to the order of the text the book incident would be placed in his twelfth year or later, but no argument can be based on the order of Asser's materials (cp. Int. p. xxv). The conclusion would appear to be that (i) Alfred was unable to read Anglo-Saxon until his twelfth year or later. (ii) That at some date prior to his second visit to Rome he showed his anxiety to learn by learning a "book" by heart. (iii) That this book was presented to him by Osburh. The negligence would appear to have date after Ethelwulf's visit to Rome, as a "master" is mentioned in the text—unless, however, the view of the repudiation of Osburh be held (cp. *supra*, note to p. 3), in which case there would be more point to Alfred's lament that in his childhood he had no masters, and later on had no time to learn (cp. p. 20).

Page 19. *The Daily Course.* That is, the prayers, psalms and lessons for the various hours of the day, on which see Honorius of Autun, *Gemma Animae* (lib. ii. *de horis canonicis* : in Migne, Pat. Lat. Vol. 172, col. 615 *et seq.*).

Ibid. Collected in one book. For further reference to this book of private devotions, cp. *infra*, p. 70. It is to be distinguished from the Handbook prepared by Asser under the king's directions (cp. *infra, loc. cit.*).

Page 20. *Occupied day and night*, etc. For a discussion of the question of the illnesses of Alfred, see Introduction, p. xlviii, and *infra* (p. 50 and notes). It may here be remarked that the "day and night without ceasing," a favourite expression with Asser, may be regarded either as mere exaggeration, as an attempt to emphasise the heroic perseverance of the king, or as an interpolation to justify the later account of his illnesses.

Page 20. *Nor, as I think, will he.* Literally, the passage would mean that Alfred, the author thought, had not faltered in his pursuit of learning to the day of his death. But the rendering here given seems to contain the meaning of Asser. Stevenson (*op. cit.,* p. 22 and p. cxxii) rejects the phrase on the ground that it bears the marks of having been added at a later date. It seems quite as likely that Asser became a little mixed in his construction of a somewhat clumsy sentence. On Alfred's zeal for learning, the *St. Albans Chronicle* (Matt. Paris, *Chron. Maj.,* I. 405) says, " for he had heard from his master that an unlearned king is an ass crowned."

Ibid. How the pagans attacked Northumbria. This passage is based on the *Chronicle* (s. a.).

Ibid. To the city of York. The *St. Albans Chronicle* (Matt. Paris, *Chron. Maj.,* I. 393, and note i. 394) tells a story about Regnar Lodbrok being wrecked on the coast of East Anglia, where he was murdered by Berno, the king's huntsman. Berno was therefore sent to sea alone in Regnar's boat, reached Denmark, and roused Regnar's sons, Ingwar and Hubba, to attack Edmund of East Anglia. In the *Saga of Lodbrok,* that king is murdered in Northumbria, but his date is put a century earlier than this attack. Hamsfort (Langbek, *Scrip. Dan.,* I. 36) makes him the victim of Ella of Northumbria in 854 or 865, but quotes no authority. The suggestion is that it was his death which led his sons to attack England. In *Gaimar* (v. 2590 *et seq.*) we find another story of a noble who, in revenge for the rape of his wife by King " Codrinus," invites the Danes to attack Northumbria. Lappenberg (*op. cit.,* II. 20 *et seq.*) inclines to accept this last story as giving us the name of Guthrum, and suggests that his attack was independent of that of Ingwar and Hubba. But Gaimar's story is too like that of the last king of the Visigoths. We have no evidence of any special cause for the attack of 867, and possibly the desire for plunder is sufficient reason for the attack. Simeon of Durham (*Hist. Dun. Ecc.* in Works, ed. Arnold, I. 54) gives a list of the leaders of the attack on the north : Halfdene, Ingwar, Hubba, Bacsecg, Guthrum, Oscytel, Amund, the two Sidrocs, Osbern Frena, and Harald. (Cp. with the list of the leaders who fell at Ashdown, pp. 28-9 ; it will be seen that Simeon makes Osbern and Frena one man.)

Page 21. *Osbert.* He succeeded to the throne in 850, on the murder

of Ethelred, and was expelled in 863. (Cp. *Sim. Dun.*, I. 53–54.)
Simeon declares that the misfortunes of both Osbert and Ella were
due to the wrath of Saint Cuthbert, whose property they had appro-
priated (*Sim. Dun.*, I. 201–202; *Hist. St. Cuth.*, I. 55; *Hist.
Dun. Ecc.*).

Page 22. *Ealhstan*. He was bishop of Sherborne from 824 to 867
(cp. *Chronicle*, s. a. 823, and notes, *Earle and Plummer*, II. 71, and
s. a. 867). His episcopate thus lasted forty-three years, not forty as
in the text, or fifty as in William of Malmesbury (*Gest. Reg.*, I.
108–109; *Gest. Pont.* 175 ff), and other authorities. In Malmesbury (*loc. cit.*) we have an account of his great power during the
reign of Ethelwulf. He thought that the king was too weak to
resist the Danes, and therefore combined with Swithun to direct the
government. Ealhstan supplied him with money and commanded
his troops with great success. He also ruled his see well, but was
avaricious and robbed Malmesbury. His generosity mitigated this
fault. Owing to his ability the reign of Ethelwulf was a success.
In the *Chronicle* we find him (*s. a.* 823) sent by Egbert to secure
Kent, and (*s. a.* 845) commanding part of the army which defeated
the Danes at the mouth of the Parret. It may be noted that on
this occasion he was acting in conjunction with Eanwulf, ealdorman
of Somerset, with whom he also conspired against Ethelwulf (see
supra, p. 8, and notes). Stevenson (*op. cit.*, p. 227) suggests that
Asser's praise of Ealhstan, which is an addition to the *Chronicle*,
may be due to a successor's gratitude for his strong rule of his see.
But it would hardly appear that Asser was bishop of Sherborne at
the time at which he was writing the *Life of Alfred*, as he does not
mention that Alfred granted it to him when recording the king's
generosity.

Ibid. How Alfred married. Asser supplies us with the only
account which we have of the marriage of Alfred.

Ibid. Recognised heir. Secundarius. The translation in the text
is derived from Plummer (*op. cit.*, p. 89 and notes). It appears to
be more probable than the alternative translations of "subregulus,"
"sub-king" (Freeman, *D. N. B.*, "Alfred"), or the "Prinzen der
Westsachsen" of Pauli (*op. cit.*, p. 91). On the other hand, in the
account of the battle of Ashdown "Secundarius" seems to mean
"second-in-command."

Page 22. *A wife from Mercia.* Elswitha. The object of the marriage of Alfred with a Mercian lady was, no doubt, like that of his sister to Burhred, to strengthen the bonds of union between Mercia and Wessex. Elswitha's name is supplied by the *Chronicle* (MS. A, *s. a.* 905 ; MS. C, *s. a.* 902). Florence of Worcester (*s. a.* 905, ed. Thorpe, p. 120) says that she founded a nunnery at Winchester. She witnesses charters of Edward the Elder up to 901. For the grant to her in Alfred's will, cp. note to p. 13. She received Wantage, Ashdown and Lamoburn. She died in 905.

Ibid. Ealdorman of the Gaini, Ethelred, surnamed Mucill. The situation of the Gaini cannot be identified with Gainsborough, as it was by Pauli (*op. cit.,* p. 92, note 1 ; cp. *Earle and Plummer, op. cit.,* II. 117), and is unknown. We know nothing of Ethelred Mucill, though a "Mucel dux" appears as witness to charters of Berhtwulf of Mercia (cp. Birch, Nos. 152, 428, 430, 432, 436, 454). Mucill has been taken to mean "the Great" (Pauli, *op. cit.,* p. 92), but Stevenson (*op. cit.,* p. 230) rejects this explanation.

Ibid. Eadburh. Nothing else is known of her.

Ibid. How Ethelred and Alfred, etc. This passage is based on the *Chronicle,* s. a.

Page 23. *Burhred.* Cp. *supra,* p. 6, and note ; *infra,* p. 32, and note.

Ibid. How the pagans ravaged England. Based on the *Chronicle,* s. a.

Page 24. *Twenty-first from the birth of King Alfred.* It will be noticed that under both 869 and 870 Alfred is described as being in his twenty-first year. According to the birth-date given by Asser we should read "twenty-second" under 870 (cp. *supra,* note to p. 1). This error of one year continues until 876 inclusive, when it is increased to an error of three years (cp. *loc. cit.* and *infra,* note to p. 37).

Ibid. Edmund. The historical facts about Edmund are scanty. He was king of the East Angles, and was defeated by the Danes in 870, either falling in the battle or being slain afterwards (*Chronicle,* s. a. 870). The principal *Life* of Saint Edmund is that by Abbo of Fleury, the *Passio Sancti Eadmundi* (Arnold, *Memorials of Saint Edmund's Abbey,* I. 3–25), which is dedicated to Dunstan and was composed under his supervision. For an account of the legend of Saint Edmund, cp. Arnold (*op. cit.*, p. **xv–xxi**). The name of his father, King Alcmund, and the other "facts" rest upon no sort of evidence. In Arnold (*op. cit.*) will be found collected most of the legendary material concerning the saint. Ingulf (ed. Birch, p. 32 *et seq.*) gives a detailed account of the Danish attack on East Anglia and Mercia which may well contain many elements of truth. The *St. Albans Chronicle* (Matt. Paris, *Chron. Maj.*, I. 392 *et seq.*) has an account of the destruction of the monasteries by the Danes and of the death of Edmund, which is peculiar to it.

Page 24. *Ceolnoth.* Archbishop from 830 to 870 (cp. *Chronicle*, s. a.). He is said to have introduced secular clerks into Christ Church, Canterbury (*Chronicle*, MS. F, *s. a.* 870).

Ibid. How the pagans, etc. From the *Chronicle*, s. a.

Ibid. Twenty-second. This should be twenty-third (cp. *supra*, note to p. 24).

Page 25. *Digged a trench.* Asser alone tells us of this action on the part of the Danes, but it was a common practice of the Danes to protect their camps in this way.

Ibid. Right-hand side. That is, on the southern side. The Welshman always looked across the Severn towards England, and so the south is on his right-hand side. Asser's use of this essentially Welsh expression is one of the many indications of the Welsh origin of the work. It may, perhaps, be added that it also shows that the work was not primarily intended for English readers, to whom this expression would presumably have been rather strange.

Ibid. How the Christians, etc. This and the succeeding passages are based on the *Chronicle*. For the variations, cp. notes to pp. 26 ff.

Ibid. Ethelwulf. (Cp. *supra*, p. 16.) He was killed at the battle of Reading (p. 26).

Ibid. The pagans gained the victory. Gaimar (v. 2964–2973), in his account of the battle, says that the Saxon army only escaped by crossing the river at Twyford by a ford of which the Danes knew nothing. Plummer (*op. cit.*, p. 93) thinks that this sounds like a genuine story.

Page 26. *Ashdown.* Æscesdun. The site of this battle would seem to be clearly identified. (Cp. *Earle and Plummer*, op. cit., II. 87–88.)

Page 26. *Shield-walls.* In the *Chronicle* there is no reference to the formation of the armies. The shield-wall (a translation for Asser's "testudo") was "only a line of shielded warriors" (cp. Oman, *Art of War*, p. 98).

Ibid. How Alfred came first to the battle. The story of the piety of Ethelred rests on the authority of Asser alone. In the *Chronicle* (MS. A, cp. MS. E, *s. a.*) the account is as follows: "And four nights from then King Ethelred and Alfred, his brother, fought with the whole 'here' at Ashdown, and the latter were in two divisions, in the one were Bacsecg and Halfdene, the heathen kings, and in the other were the jarls; and then King Ethelred fought with the king's followers, and there was King Bacsecg slain; and Alfred, his brother, fought with the followers of the jarls, and there was Jarl Sidroc the Elder slain, and Jarl Sidroc the Younger, and Jarl Osbern, and Jarl Frena, and Jarl Harald, and both armies were put to flight (*al.* he put both armies to flight), and there were many thousands slain, and they continued fighting until night." (It is to be noted that the old English text is here slightly ambiguous, as "gefliemde" may be either the third person singular or the participle, and "hergas" either subject or object.) *Florence of Worcester* (*s. a.* 871, ed. Thorpe, I. 83–84) copies Asser literally, but adds, after describing the entry of Alfred into the battle, "At last King Ethelred, having made an end of the prayers in which he was absorbed, arrived, and having called upon the great King of the World, forthwith gave himself to the fight." Stevenson (*op. cit.,* p. 30) adds the passage from *Florence* (incidentally giving "magni mundi principe" for the "magno mundi principe" of the printed text of *Florence*). Plummer (*op. cit.,* p. 93–94) finds it hard to accept the story, but suggests that, if it be true, then the late arrival of Ethelred may have contributed to the victory. It seems that there is no reason to doubt the story. The compiler of the *Chronicle* and Asser were about equally well placed for the securing of definite information on such a matter, and it is not an extravagant assumption that Asser may have received his account directly from Alfred. The detail into which he enters is indicative of the importance of the event in his eyes, and it is quite possible that he would have asked the king for details on an event which made so great an impression on him. This being so, it seems that it is at least possible that Asser has preserved the true account of the battle. In the *Chronicle* we have the plan which was formed for the battle, a plan also given by Asser. The compiler of the *Chronicle* was not aware of the modification of the plan owing to the slowness of Ethelred, and therefore implies that Ethelred took part in the battle, unless, indeed, we take "gefliemde" as singular, and as showing that the chronicler was aware that the victory was entirely due to Alfred. Asser, on the other hand, knew of the modification in the plan. The passage from *Florence* may be regarded as an attempt on the part of that compiler to reconcile the *Chronicle* and Asser. It is clear that this view cannot be proved, but if Asser is to be trusted at all, if he knew anything of the history of Wessex prior to his arrival there, he would surely know the true history of the battle of Ashdown. Any argument which is brought against his account might almost equally well be used to deny the second journey of Alfred to Rome, on which the *Chronicle* is silent, yet that account has been generally accepted. Accordingly, then, the account in Asser may well be taken as the real version, and that in the *Chronicle* as erroneous. It may be mentioned that it is noteworthy that Asser does not say that Ethelred killed Bagsecg or defeated any part of the Danish army ; and it may be added that the expression " invocato magno mundi principe " is not very like the general style of Asser, who nowhere else uses either the word "mundus " or the word " princeps."

Page 28. *A single very stuntea thorn-tree.* On this thorn-tree see the interesting note in Plummer (*op. cit.,* p. 94).

Ibid. Bacsecg, etc. Of these leaders nothing further is known, except the reference to them in *Simeon of Durham* (cp. *supra,* note to p. 20), and a possible reference to the elder Sidroc in the Frankish annals (*Chron. Fontan.,* s. a. 842, 845). Some MSS. of the *Chronicle* place the death of the elder Sidroc, or of one Sidroc, at the battle of Englefield, but this is an error (cp. *Chronicle,* MS. E, *s. a.* 871, in which MS. both Sidrocs are also killed at Ashdown).

Page 29. *How the war continued.* Cp. the *Chronicle,* s. a. It will be noticed that there is in the text no reference to the battle of Mertun. In *Florence of Worcester* (*s. a.* 871, ed. Thorpe, I. 85) we find a reference to it : "Again, when two months had passed, King Ethelred and his brother Alfred fought with the pagans, who had divided themselves into two bands, at Mertun, and for a long while were victors, and all their adversaries were turned in flight ; but they returned to the battle and many fell on both sides, and the pagans gained the victory and held the place of slaughter." Plummer (*op. cit.*, p. 23, note 1) suggests that this passage has been omitted from Asser "merely owing to homoioteleuton " : the words "pagani victoria" recurring. Stevenson does not include the passage in his text of Asser, but appears inclined to think that it was not really omitted (*op. cit.*, p. 239–240). Plummer's explanation certainly would appear to be almost conclusive.

Page 29. *Ethelred . . . went the way of all flesh.* Florence of Worcester (*loc. cit.*) gives the date as April 23.

Ibid. How Alfred began to reign. There is every reason to suppose that the succession of Alfred was in accordance with an agreement with his brother, so far as the will of his brother could have any influence, as he was to succeed to the personal property of the king (cp. note to p. 13), so he was "secundarius," recognised as heir to the throne (cp. note to p. 22). The reason for this is to be found in the troubled condition of England, for Ethelred left at least one son. A son Ethelwald is mentioned in the *Chronicle* (*s. a.* 901) as rebelling against Edward the Elder, and was killed in an attempt to rouse the East Anglian Danes against his cousin (*Chronicle*, s. a. 905). It is probable that Ethelwerd, the historian, was descended from another son ; in any case he was descended from Ethelred. In his dedication (*M. H. B.*, 499 C), and on two other occasions (514 A, and 514 B), he mentions that Ethelred was his ancestor. It may be presumed that these sons were minors in 871, though they may have been the people who raised questions as to Alfred's disposal of his inherited property at a later date (cp. note to p. 13).

Page 30. *Even while that brother*, etc. Plummer (*op. cit.*, p. 86) suggests that the meaning of this is that Alfred might have asserted his claim to the sub-kingdom of Kent.

Ibid. How Alfred first fought the pagans. This passage is based on the *Chronicle* (*s. a.* 871).

Page 31. *Eight battles.* In the *Chronicle* (*s. a.* 871) nine pitched battles (folcgefeoht) are mentioned as having occurred in this year, of which the names of six are given : Englefield, Reading, Ashdown, Basing, Mertun and Wilton. Asser has five of these, and an account of the sixth (Mertun) should probably be added (cp. *supra*, note to p. 29). Ethelwerd (*M. H. B.*, 513 C D E; 514 C) mentions the victory of Ethelwulf, *i. e.* Englefield, the battles of Reading, Ashdown, Basing and Mertun, and a second battle at Reading. The second battle of Reading may be an error for Wilton, but it is also possible, as Plummer (*op. cit.*, p. 98) suggests, that Ethelwerd has preserved for us the name of another battle.

Page 31. *The Saxons made an agreement.* The *Chronicle* (*s. a.*) mentions the conclusion of an agreement, but does not mention the terms.

Ibid. How the pagans, etc. These passages are based on the *Chronicle* (*s. a.* 872, 873, 874).

Ibid. Twenty-third. This should be twenty-fourth (cp. *supra*, note to p. 24).

Page 32. *Twenty-fourth.* This should be twenty-fifth (cp. *supra loc. cit.*).

Ibid. Lindsey. The *Chronicle*, MS. A (*s. a.* 873), adds Torksey; MS. E omits Lindsey.

Ibid. How King Burhred, etc. Based on the *Chronicle* (*s. a.* 874). For Burhred (cp. *supra*, pp. 6, 23 and notes to p. 6). Ethelswith did not go with him, but stayed with her brother, Alfred (Will. Malm., *Gesta Regum*, I. 96). At a later date she followed him but died at Pavia (Will. Malm., *loc. cit.*). Her death is recorded in the *Chronicle* (*s. a.* 888). The *St. Albans Chronicle* (Matt. Paris, *Chron. Maj.*, I. 427) says that she died a nun, and places her death in 890 : probably in error.

Ibid. The School of the Saxons. Gregorovius, (*Hist. of the City of Rome in the Middle Ages* : Eng. trans. Vol. II. 422 *et seq.*) points out that the "scholae" originated from the organisation of the imperial household troops under Diocletian, and the later organisation of the militia of the city of Rome. The "scholae perigrinorum" were not essentially educational establishments, but corporations or guilds of foreigners : they appear to have been more of a mediæval substitute for the consulate of to-day. There were "schools" of the Saxons, Franks, Lombards and Frisians. The Anglo-Saxon was the oldest. Gregorovius (p. 425) holds that it was founded by Ine in 727, with a church for the burial of Saxons who might die at Rome, and a place for religious instruction : that it was restored and enlarged by Offa. The date of foundation is not known, however, and Offa has also been named as its founder (cp. *supra*, notes to pp. 2, 11). It was burnt under Paschalis, and again under Leo IV (cp. *Lib. Pont.*, II. 53, 110–111). It was restored by Ethelwulf on the occasion of his visit to Rome (Will. Malm. *Gesta Regum*, I. 109). The *St. Albans Chronicle* (Matt. Paris, *Chron. Maj.*, I. 330–331) says that after its foundation by Ine it was deprived of its wealth by the greed of the Romans, which was the reason why Offa found it necessary to restore it.

Page 33. *Ceowulf.* The account here is based on the *Chronicle* (*s. a.* 874, MS. E). William of Malmesbury (*Gesta Regum*, I. 96) declares that Mercia was exhausted under his rule. In Ingulf (ed. Birch, p. 45–46) he is called "an Englishman by birth, but from his impiety a barbarian." A description of the exactions to which he was driven by the demands of the Danes follows. Croyland had to pay a thousand pounds, and so forth. Amid a mass of exaggeration and fiction it is not impossible that a substratum of truth is preserved, and that the Danes made Ceowulf king in the hope that he would find it more easy to exact money for them than they would to exact it for themselves.

Ibid. How the army of the pagans was divided. This passage is based on the *Chronicle* (*s. a.* 875). It may be noted that in the fact of this division of the army one cause of the ultimate success of Alfred may be found. The whole force of the Danes was no longer concentrated on Wessex.

Ibid. Twenty-sixth. This should be twenty-seventh (cp. *supra*, p. 24).

Ibid. Halfdene. He was the brother of Ingwar and Hubba, and one of the sons of Regnar Lodbrok (cp. above, p. 20 note).

Ibid. Into the land of the Northumbrians. The land was ravaged unmercifully, and the monks of Lindisfarne fled with the body of Saint Cuthbert to Chester-le-Street. (Cp. *Sim. Dun.*, I. 56–58, and in *Hist. St. Cuth.*, I. 207, 208, 235.)

Ibid. Picts . . . men of Strathclyde. Ethelwerd (515 A) calls the latter, Cumbri : the first instance of this name. The war with the Picts is mentioned in the Irish annals (cp. *Earle and Plummer*, op. cit., II. 90).

Ibid. Guthrum. As to the mention of Guthrum earlier by Simeon of Durham, and as to the alleged cause of his attack on England, see *supra* (note to p. 20). Nothing is known of his previous history. In the *War of the Gaedhill with the Gaill* (ed. Todd, p. 266) there is a genealogy of Guthrum, " Gormo Enske " ; he is called the son of Frotho : but there is no foundation for the genealogy.

Page 33. *Six ships.* The *Chronicle* (*s. a.*) has seven.

Page 34. *How the pagans,* etc. Based on the *Chronicle*, s. a. 876.

Ibid. Twenty-seventh. This should be twenty-eighth (cp. *supra*, note to p. 24).

Ibid. A fortress, called Wareham. There are still traces of the old fortifications (Plummer, *op. cit.*, p. 100).

Ibid. Monastery of nuns. Nothing is known of this nunnery (cp. *Monasticon*, VI. iii. 1617 : ed. 1844). "An ancient monastery, probably the earliest religious foundation in this county, was built here in Saxon times, but afterwards destroyed in the Danish raid of 876." (*Victoria Hist. : Dorset,* II. 121.)

Ibid. Durngueis. Stevenson (*op. cit.*, p. 250) gives Durngueir as the true reading.

Ibid. Thornsaeta. The usual form was Dornsæte, and the form in the text is not found elsewhere (Stevenson, *loc. cit.*).

Ibid. Sure agreement. Ethelwerd (515 B) says that the peace was bought, and this would appear to be an addition to the information contained in the *Chronicle* and in Asser.

Ibid. Swearing an oath. The value of an oath sworn by pagans on the relics of saints is not at first sight very obvious. Lappenberg (*op. cit.*, II. 49, note 4) suggests that the explanation is to be found not in the credulity of Alfred, but in the fact that the bones of the dead were held in veneration by the northern nations. In the *Chronicle* (*s. a.* 876) it is the "halig beah," the sacred ring, on which the oath is taken (for which cp. *Earle and Plummer*, op. cit., II. 90–91). It may be suggested that Asser has confused an oath on an object sacred to the Danes with one on an object sacred to the Christians, or that the oath was confirmed by the sacred objects of both religions. It might be that Alfred feared that the Danes would not regard an oath as binding unless it was confirmed in a manner which might seem to bind both parties.

Ibid. Dispatched all the horsemen. In the text we have " slew all the horsemen " (equites, *not* equos) "which it had." An emendation, suggested by Florence of Worcester, made the passage read, "which the king had." The passage has thus been taken to mean either that the Danes killed their horses (which is in no case what the Latin says), or that they annihilated a body of cavalry belonging to Alfred, of which there is no mention in the *Chronicle*. In the *Chronicle* we have "The mounted part of the army escaped from the 'fyrd' to Exeter." In the passage interpolated from the *Annals of Saint Neot* (*infra*, p. 36) we have the same idea : "The army of the heathen left Wareham, some on horseback, some in ships." In *Henry of Huntingdon* (p. 146) we have, "On the next night, those of the army who had horses departed by stealth and went to Exeter." It is thus fairly clear that the text is corrupt, while taken literally it makes nonsense, as Florence seems to have felt when he added "rex." In the present translation the alternative reading given in the *Monumenta* has been taken.

Page 34. *Exeter*. The Danish army would seem to have reached Exeter in 877 (cp. *Chronicle*, s. a. 876 and 877). This is the first mention of Exeter in history (Freeman, *Exeter*, p. 20).

Page 35. *The whole land of the Northumbrians*. As a matter of fact the Danes only occupied Deira. In Bernicia an English kingdom persisted (cp. *Earle and Plummer*, II. 91, and for the chronology, *ibid.*, p. 85).

Ibid. How Rollo, etc. For a note on this and on the following interpolated passage, cp. *infra* (notes on interpolations, p. 148).

Page 36. *How the pagans divided Mercia*. This passage is based on the *Chronicle* (*s. a.* 877). It has been suggested that here we have the origin of the division of Mercia between the English and the Danes, which received final confirmation after the battle of Edington (Green, *Conquest of England*, p. 106). It may be presumed that western Mercia was left to Ceolwulf, since that it was less ravaged than the eastern part is seen from the fact that it was to western Mercia that Alfred sent for his scholars (cp. *infra*, p. 57, and note).

Page 37. *How the pagans came to Chippenham*. This passage is based on the *Chronicle*, s. a.

Ibid. Twenty-seventh. This should be thirtieth. It will be noticed that the age is repeated from the annal for 876, which increases the error from one year to two years, and that the annal for 877 has been omitted in the genuine text of Asser, so that another year is added to the error, making three years in all. During the rest of the annalistic portion of Asser this error is maintained.

Page 37. *Left-hand.* That is, northern (cp. *supra*, note to p. 25, and Introduction, p. xxvii).

Ibid. Abon. The river Avon.

Ibid. How Alfred abode in Athelney. Athelney is at the junction of the Tone and Parrett (cp. *Earle and Plummer,* op. cit., II. 93). There is no doubt that Alfred spent his time of retirement here in organising the renewal of the war, and there is no ground for regarding him as a despairing refugee (cp. *supra*, Introduction, p. x, and *infra*, p. 38 *et seq.*, and note). For the story of the vision of Saint Cuthbert and of Alfred as a harper, cp. William of Malmesbury (*Gest. Reg.*, II. 125 and 126).

Ibid. Vassals. A Frankish word ; " vasalus " means " member of his household " : its use here shows the Frankish element in Asser.

Page 38. *The story of the burning of the cakes.* Cp. *infra*, notes on interpolations, p. 148.

Ibid. How Alfred merited his misfortunes. Cp. Introduction, p. xlvii, and notes on interpolations, p. 148. This passage is that which is most typical of the legendary Alfred.

Page 40. *How the pagans were beaten in North Devon.* This passage is based on the *Chronicle*, s. a. 878.

Ibid. The brother of Ingwar and Halfdene. This is possibly Hubba. His name is not supplied by the *Chronicle*.

Ibid. Dyfed. Demetia, or South Wales. The fact that the Danish army had wintered there before coming to Devon is given only by Asser, and may be taken as one of the indications of the Welsh character of the work.

Ibid. Cynwit. This is usually identified with Kenny Castle near Appledore (cp. *Earle and Plummer*, op. cit., II. 93, and Stevenson, *op. cit.*, p. 262 *et seq.*). Ethelwerd (515 D E) gives the name of the English leader as Odda, and says that the Danes none the less took the fortress. Its fate is nowhere else mentioned.

Ibid. A thousand and two hundred. The *Chronicle* agrees with Asser ; Ethelwerd (515 E) gives eight hundred as the number of slain.

Ibid. After our fashion. This would appear to mean in the manner of the Welsh, that is, the fortification was of a very rudimentary character.

Page 41. *How the Raven Banner was taken.* Cp. *infra,* notes on interpolations, p. 149.

Ibid. How Alfred came forth from Athelney. This passage is based on the *Chronicle.*

Ibid. With the chief men of Somerset. This passage is an indication of the way in which Alfred was spending his time in reorganising his army.

Ibid. Egbert's stone. The identification of this place is uncertain.

Ibid. All the people of the districts, etc. This would seem to show that the advance of Alfred was prearranged (cp. Plummer, *op. cit.,* p. 102).

Page 42. *They were filled with joy.* In the *Chronicle* (*s. a.* 878), "ond his gefaegene waerun," "they were fain of him." As Plummer (*op. cit., loc. cit.*) says, the simplicity of the expression is testimony to the sincerity of the feeling.

Ibid. How Alfred came to Edington, etc. This passage is based on the *Chronicle* (*s. a.* 878).

Ibid. Aecglea. Identification is uncertain.

Ibid. Edington. Ethandun. The identification of Ethandun with Edington seems to be comparatively well established.

Ibid. Shield-wall. Cp. *supra,* note to p. 26.

Ibid. How the pagans submitted, etc. Based on the *Chronicle* (*s. a.* 878).

Page 43. *The pagans also swore that they would straightway depart from his realm.* The agreement which was on this occasion made between Alfred and Guthrum is not to be confused with the later "Alfred and Guthrum's Peace," of which the text is preserved (cp. Thorpe, *Ancient Laws,* etc., I. 152 *et seq.*) : it was probably concluded in 886 (cp. *Earle and Plummer,* op. cit., II. 94–95, 99–100, and *infra,* note to p. 49). On the present occasion, the peace of Wedmore, no terms as to the division of England are recorded, and it seems probable that no such terms were made. The Danes were to leave Wessex—that was all. Actually, they left western Mercia also, and retired to East Anglia, which had been so long under Danish control that it was naturally better suited for colonisation.

Ibid. Guthrum . . . promised that he would accept Christianity.

There is no indication here or elsewhere in the text that the conversion was more than a personal one. The *Chronicle* also has no hint of a national conversion. On a later occasion Asser still describes the subjects of Guthrum as " pagans " (*infra*, p. 47). On the other hand, it is at least probable that some of the Danes followed their king's example, and that Alfred was partly moved to insist on conversion as a means of dividing the Danes against themselves. Guthrum and his army would form a kind of buffer state between Wessex and the northern Danes.

Page 43. *Seven weeks*. In the *Chronicle*, three weeks.

Ibid. His son by adoption. Guthrum took the additional name of Athelstan (cp. *Chronicle*, s. a. 890).

Ibid. Chrism-loosing. A newly baptised child wore a fillet bound round its head ; loosing this was the chrism-loosing, and took place a week after the baptism (Bede, ed. Plummer, II. 280).

Ibid. Articles of goldsmiths' work. Aedificia. The translation is Plummer's, and for an explanation of it cp. Plummer (*op. cit.*, p. 46).

Ibid. How the Pagans left the land of the West Saxons. This is based on the *Chronicle* (*s. a.* 879–880).

Ibid. Twenty-eighth. This should be thirty-first (cp. *supra*, note to p. 37).

Page 44. *Hwiccas.* They were a tribe in Worcestershire and Gloucestershire. They are mentioned in the *Chronicle* (*s. a.* 800). The district was under an ealdorman, and was apparently a small kingdom or sub-kingdom before the unification of Mercia.

Ibid. An army of the pagans. This army was commanded by Hasting (cp. Lappenberg, *op. cit.*, 55 and note 2).

Ibid. An eclipse of the sun. Plummer (*Earle and Plummer*, op. cit., II. 95) suggests that Asser has here altered the hour of the eclipse to make it fit his chronology. There was an eclipse in 878 and another in 879, but the former was the more important. It is therefore suggested that the events here recorded really belong to the year 878.

Ibid. Twenty-ninth. This should be thirty-second (cp. *supra*, note to p. 37).

Ibid. How the heathen warred in the land of the Franks. This passage is based on the *Chronicle*, s.a. 881, 882, 883. For a suggested reason for the incorporation of these details in the *Life* cp. Introduction, p. xxviii *et seq.*

Page 44. *Thirtieth.* This should be thirty-third (cp. *supra*, p. note to p. 37).

Page 45. *The Franks fought against it.* This battle has been identified with that of Saucourt, in which Lewis III defeated the Northmen (Lappenberg, *op. cit.*, II. 56 ; Regino, *Chronicle*, s. a. 883).

Ibid. Thirty-first. This should be thirty-fourth (cp. *supra*, p. 37, note).

Ibid. A battle with ships. Lappenberg (*op. cit.*, II. 58) traces this Danish attack to the treaty made by Lewis III with Hasting.

Ibid. Thirty-second. This should be thirty-fifth (cp. *supra*).

Ibid. Monastery of nuns. Asser adds this detail to the account in the *Chronicle*.

Page 46. *How the pagans attacked Rochester.* This passage is based on the *Chronicle*, s. a. 885.

Ibid. Thirty-third. This should be thirty-sixth (cp. *supra*, p. 37, note).

Ibid. Into East Francia. Ethelwerd (516) names Louvain as the district into which the Danes went.

Ibid. How Alfred sent his fleet against East Anglia. The passage is based on the *Chronicle* (*s. a.* 885). The cause of this expedition, given by Asser merely as "to take booty," would seem to be that the East Anglian Danes had given help to the Danes who attacked Rochester. It would seem that the passage (on p. 49) as to the breach of the peace by the Danes should more properly come before the account of this expedition. That Alfred's fleet went from Kent seems to connect this operation with those of the siege of Rochester.

Page 47. *About to return home.* In the text we have "dormiret," a clear error for "domum iret" (cp. Plummer, *op. cit.*, p. 64). The *Chronicle* has "hamweard wendon." Simeon of Durham (II. 87)— which is really the Cuthbertine monk—bases a moral lesson on the misreading ; the genuine Simeon (II. 117) restores the true reading, as does *Florence of Worcester* (ed. Thorpe, I. 100).

Ibid. Concerning the affairs of the Frankish kingdom. This is based on the *Chronicle*, s. a. 885.

Ibid. Carloman. King of Burgundy and Aquitaine, 879 ; king of

the West Franks, 882.   He was the son of Lewis II by Ansgarde.
There is a story that he was really accidentally killed by one of his
attendants (*Earle and Plummer*, II. 97).   For his death, which
occurred on Dec. 12, 884, see Regino (*Chronicle*, s. a. 884).   It may
be noted that Asser corrects the *Chronicle* in two respects : he gives
Carloman for the " Carl " of the *Chronicle*, and he adds " West "
before Franks.

Page 47. *His brother Lewis.*   Lewis III, king of Neustria, 879–
882 ; son of Lewis II. and Ansgarde, elder brother of Carloman
(cp. Regino, *s. a.* 883).

Ibid. Lewis, king of the Franks.   Son of Charles the Bald, and king
of the West Franks, 877–879.   He was the victor of Saucourt, and
was surnamed " the Stammerer."

Ibid. Charles.   Cp. *supra*, note to p. 8.

Page 48. *From Germany.*   Plummer (*op. cit.*, p. 40–41) says that
this means Scandinavia ; since Asser nowhere applies it to any part
of the Frankish kingdom, and since the Danes could hardly be said to
go " from Germany " into Saxony.   On the other hand, Asser might
have drawn such a distinction owing to his misunderstanding Einhard
(*Vita Karoli Magni*, c. 15), where we find, " the part of Germany
between Saxony and the Danube," and have regarded Einhard as
drawing a distinction between the two.

Ibid. Saxons and Frisians.   For these battles, cp. *Annals of Fulda*
(*s. a.* 884).

Ibid. Charles, king of the Alamanni.   Charles III, the Fat, was
the third son of Lewis the German.   He received the kingdom of
the Alamanni, 876, on his father's death ; secured Italy on the
death of Lewis the Stammerer, in 879, by agreement with his
brothers.   The successive deaths of his brothers, Carloman (880)
and Lewis (882), left him the whole of the East Frankish kingdom,
and in 885 he succeeded to the West Frankish kingdom also on the
death of Carloman, king of the West Franks, to the exclusion of
Charles the Simple, the only surviving son of Lewis the Stammerer.
Meanwhile he had been crowned emperor by Pope John VIII in
881.   Thus he reunited the whole of the empire of Charles the
Great, with the exception of Armorica, where the Bretons maintained their independence, and of the kingdom of Boso (cp. *infra*,
note to p. 68).

Page 48. *Mediterranean Sea.* Mare Terrenum in Asser. In the *Chronicle*, Wendel sæ (*s. a.* 885).

Ibid. Lewis, who was brother to Charles. Lewis the German, king of Austrasia, or of the East Franks, 840–876 ; son of Lewis the Pious by Ermengarde, and half-brother to Charles the Bald, who was the son of Lewis the Pious by his second marriage to Judith.

Ibid. Charles. Charles the Great, king of the Franks, 768 ; emperor, 800–814.

Ibid. Pippin. Pippin the Short, king of the Franks, 751–768, the founder of the Carolingian dynasty.

Ibid. Marinus. Pope Marinus I, 882–884. There is an account of his gifts to Alfred in the *Chronicle* (MS. A, *s. a.* 885 ; MS. E, *s. a.* 883, 885), on which Asser's account is based. Hincmar (*Ann.*, s. a. 864) mentions a riot at Rome on the occasion of the visit of Charles the Bald, in which the cross made by Helena, mother of Constantine the Great, was broken in pieces. Some of the pieces were, " as it is said," saved by certain Englishmen, and it may be that the gifts of Marinus were intended to mark the papal gratitude, though some years were allowed to pass before they were made. For the gifts, cp. Kemble (*Codex Dipl.*, No. DCCCXXIV), and *Monasticon* (I. 293–295 : No. IV. ed. 1844) in the first charter of Edward the Confessor to Westminster.

Page 49. *How the pagans of East Anglia broke the peace.* Cp. *supra*, note to p. 46.

Ibid. How the author, etc. This is the second occasion on which Asser explains the proposed contents of the book (cp. *supra*, p. 18) ; it will be noticed that here also he does not tell us his object (cp. Introduction, p. xxix).

Ibid. Life and manners, etc. This passage is based on Einhard (*Vita Karoli Magni*, Preface), where we find, " the life and conversation, and in no small degree the acts, of my lord and protector," etc. And again, " endeavouring neither to pass by any of those matters which have been able to come to my knowledge, nor to weary the minds of those who are hard to please by any excessive detail in my account " (cp. Introduction, p. xxvi).

Ibid. As I have promised. This presumably refers to his previous declaration that he would not be too prolix (cp. *supra*, p. 18).

Ibid. How Alfred fell ill at the time of his wedding. It will be noticed that Asser, after carrying the annalistic part of his work down to 884, suddenly goes back to the year 868. This illustrates his peculiar arrangement, but in the present instance it would seem that he was now anxious to reach the account of his own relations with the king, since he had reached the year in which those relations began ; it was therefore necessary to deal with all the intervening incidents in Alfred's life.

Page 50. From his twentieth year, etc. Cp. *infra*, note to p. 50, and Introduction, p. xxviii, for reasons for regarding this assertion of the perpetual illness of Alfred as rather exaggerated.

Ibid. Applause and devotion of the people. The allusion would seem to be to Acts xii. 22, 23.

Ibid. Others regarded it as being the ficus. There is no necessary inconsistency between this passage and the later declaration that the ficus was removed in answer to his prayer. Asser implies that those who thought this were wrong ; they were under the impression that the illness was a return of the complaint from which Alfred had suffered in the past.

Ibid. Concerning the earlier illnesses of Alfred. This passage has been generally given as part of the genuine Asser, but it is admitted that it is confused and corrupted, and that some part of it is probably interpolated. It has been already suggested (Int., p. xlviii *et seq.*) that there is reason for regarding the whole passage as interpolated ; those reasons may be here elaborated. In the first place the account is very confused ; it makes the following statements—

i. Alfred suffered from the ficus from infancy (p. 50).

ii. The ficus was given him in answer to prayer, in the first flower of his youth (p. 51–52).

iii. The ficus was removed in answer to prayer (p. 50–51).

iv. The illness which struck him at the time of his wedding was given him in answer to prayer as a substitute for the ficus (p. 52).

v. The illness which was to replace the ficus was to be a lighter affliction, not such as should make him incapable, for he feared leprosy and blindness (p. 51).

vi. The illness which struck him on his wedding day left him often unfit for all labour (p. 52).

It is clear that the first and second of these statements are in flat contradiction to one another, while the second illness does not answer the description of the illness for which Alfred prayed. It is fairly clear that there are here two stories jumbled together, and therefore one at least must be an interpolation. That the whole passage has merely grown out of the fact that he was ill on his wedding day, and often in ill health, seems likely on the following grounds—

i. In this passage Alfred appears as a moral coward, who dares not fight against temptation (p. 51).

ii. He appears as morbidly religious. This is not in accord with his character as elsewhere displayed, *e.g.* at the battle of Ashdown.

iii. He would hardly have been capable of the work which he accomplished if he had been perpetually in agony.

iv. He would hardly have been "merry" (cp. p. 54) if he had also been either in great agony or in mortal terror (cp. p. 52).

v. The general air of the passage is monastic; it sounds as though it might have been added under the revival of Dunstan's period.

It may be concluded, then, that this passage is an interpolation, or at least so corrupt as to be valueless; perhaps the illness of Alfred should share the fate of the burnt cakes. It would seem that either this has to be done, or we must revise our estimate of his character. As to the references to his illness elsewhere, Asser was fond of exaggeration, and the fact that Alfred was not generally in a very rude state of health would seem likely to become perpetual and severe illness in the hands of Asser; his expressions are constantly in need of toning down.

For notes on this passage, cp. notes on the interpolations, p. 149.

Page 52. *Concerning the family of King Alfred.* Of the children here mentioned some are well known. Ethelfleda is the "lady of the Mercians" who was largely responsible for the recovery of the Danelaw, ably seconding the efforts of her brother; she died in 918 (*Chronicle*, MS. E), or 922 (MS. A). Edward succeeded his father in 901 (MS. A), and died in 924. Elgiva is only known through this mention and the subsequent account of her in Asser (cp. p. 81). Elftryth became the wife of Baldwin II, count of Flanders. Ethelwerd is not otherwise known; one of the legends sends him to the University of Oxford.

Ibid. Edred. Ethelred. He died in 910–912.

Page 53. *This school.* It is not impossible that this court-school was modelled on that of Charles the Great (cp. Einhard, c. 19), and that Asser borrowed from Einhard in describing it. On the other hand, the wish expressed by Alfred in the Preface to the *Pastoral Care* is evidence that it really was the wish of the king to secure the education of his subjects.

Page 54. *Articles of goldsmiths' work.* Cp. *supra*, note to p. 43.

Ibid. Concerning the virtues of Alfred. In this, and in the ensuing passages of the *Life*, Asser draws very largely from Einhard (cp. *Vit. Kar. Mag. passim*, esp. cc. 21, 26, 27).

Page 56. *Sought first wisdom from God.* Cp. 2 Chron. i. 7–12 ; 1 Kings, iii. 5–13.

Ibid. Seek ye first, etc. Matt. vi. 33. The quotation is from the old Latin version, reading " praestabuntur " for the " adjicientur " of the Vulgate.

Ibid. I will hearken, etc. Ps. lxxxv. 8 (Vulgate, lxxxiv. 9).

Page 57. *How the king obtained helpers from Mercia.* The reason for looking to Mercia for scholars is no doubt to be found in the fact that western Mercia had suffered less from the Danes than any other part of England (cp. *supra*, note to p. 36).

Ibid. Werferth. He was bishop of Worcester, 873–915. No details are recorded of his life other than those in the text.

Ibid. Dialogues of Gregory, etc. Printed by Hecht, *Grein-Wülker, Bibliothek der angelsächsischen Prosa*, Vol. V. It is interesting that there are two versions of a large part of this work, one being in effect a revision of the other (cp. Plummer, *op. cit.*, 145–146).

Ibid. Sometimes making a paraphrase. Cp. Introduction, p. xvi. The general character of Alfred's translations is that they do not adhere at all closely to the original.

Ibid. Plegmund. He is said to have lived on an island near Chester as a hermit. Became archbishop in 890, receiving the pallium at Rome from Formosus in the next year. He is said to have tried to introduce reforms into the division of his province into sees, and to have crowned Edward the Elder. Mentioned in the Preface to the *Pastoral Care*. Visited Rome a second time under Edward the Elder. Died Aug. 2, 914. His name appears as a witness to several charters of the period (*D. N. B.*, s. n.).

Ibid. Athelstan and Werwulf. Nothing is known of these two men, though they were converted into bishops in the legend of the Middle Ages (cp. Matt. Paris, *Chron. Maj.*, I. 407), the sees of Hereford and Leicester being assigned to them. Athelstan was possibly the envoy to India, if any envoy from Alfred ever reached that country.

Page 58. *Grimbald.* He was a monk of the monastery of Saint Bertin, near Saint Omer, and became chancellor and prior. He is said to have come to Alfred about 893, received a letter of recommendation from Fulk, archbishop of Rheims. He became abbot of New-minster, Winchester, which was planned by Alfred and built by Edward the Elder (903). Grimbald died on July 8, 903. (*D. N. B.*, s. n.). For the story that Asser fetched him, cp. Introduction, p. xx.

Ibid. John the Old Saxon. Nothing is known of his life. He has been confused with John Scotus Erigena (fl. *circa* 850), who taught at the court of Charles the Bald, and was a comparatively prominent writer (works in Migne, Pat. Lat., Vol. 122). For the experiences of John as abbot of Athelney, cp. *infra*, p. 77–87.

Page 59. *How Asser came to the king.* Cp. Introduction, p. xii *et seq.*

Ibid. Right-hand Saxons. South Saxons (cp. note to p. 25).

Ibid. Dean. This is Dean near Eastbourne.

Ibid. Left-hand. That is, north (cp. *supra*, note to p. 25). On the possessions of Asser in Wales, cp. Introduction, p. xii, xviii.

Page 60. *Britain.* This is an example of the restricted sense in which Asser uses the word ; it here means Wales only.

Ibid. Winchester. Some confusion has arisen owing to the mis-understanding of this passage. The Latin would bear the meaning that Asser lay at Winchester for a year and a week ; and taking it to mean this, it has been argued that the statement proves that the *Life* is not authentic, as Asser could not have remained in Winchester for that length of time without Alfred being aware of it. To over-come the difficulty, Stevenson (*op. cit.*, p. 313, 314) has suggested that Wintonia means Caerwent. On the other hand, the relative pronoun can refer to the fever quite as well as to Winchester, and it has here been so taken.

Page 61. *The land of the Saxons.* Saxonia in the text. It has been generally translated Saxony, but such a translation gives to the dominions of Alfred a term which has been generally confined to the continental Saxony, and in the present translation this ambiguity has been deliberately avoided.

Page 61. *And the former*, etc. For the quasi-political character of Asser's residence at the court of Alfred, cp. Introduction, p. xiv. The translation of this sentence is rather conjectural.

Ibid. Saint David. He flourished in the fifth or sixth century, 446–544 being the date given by the Bollandists (*Acta SS.* March 1); he was bishop of St. David's (Menevia). Gir. Cambrensis wrote a *Life* of St. David (cp. Works, Vol. III., ed. Brewer, p. 377 *et seq.*).

Ibid. Hemeid. King of Dyfed (Pembrokeshire). His death is mentioned in the *Annales Cambriae*, s. a. 892.

Ibid. Concerning the affairs of Wales. This is another indication of the Welsh origin of the *Life*, and of the birthplace of the author (cp. Introduction, p. xii, etc.).

Ibid. Nobis. His accession to the see of St. Davids is recorded in the *Annales Cambriae*, s. a. 840, and his death, *s. a.* 873.

Ibid. Archbishop. Asser, as a Welshman, regards the see of St. Davids as the archiepiscopal see of Wales. Possibly it would be most accurate to describe the holders of the see at this period as bishops with archiepiscopal powers.

Ibid. Right-hand part of Britain. That is, South Wales.

Ibid. Demetia. South Wales.

Page 62. *Six sons of Rhodri.* For Rhodri Mawr, cp. *supra*, note to p. 5. Four surviving sons of Rhodri appear to occur in the *Annales Cambriae*—Anaraut (*s. a.* 894, 915), Merwyn (*s. a.* 903), Catell (*s. a.* 909), and Indgual (*s. a.* 943). In all these cases, except that of Anaraut (cp. *infra*), it is merely the death of each that is recorded.

Ibid. Howell ap Rhys. His death is recorded in the *Annales Cambriae* as taking place at Rome in 885, in the *Brut y Tywysogion* as taking place in 894. The latter would seem to be the true date.

Ibid. Glewissig. The modern county of Glamorgan.

Ibid. Brochmail, and Fernmail, . . kings of Gwent. Their names do not appear in the *Annales Cambriae*. A Mouric died in the same year as Nobis (*Ann. Cam.*, s. a. 873). Gwent corresponds to the modern Monmouth.

Ibid. Edred. Ethelred, Alfred's son-in-law (cp. *supra*, note to p. 52).

Page 62. *Helised ap Teudyr.* Nothing is known of him. His kingdom was the modern Brecknock.

Ibid. Anaraut. He appears in the *Annales Cambriae* under 894 as combining with the Angles (presumably Mercians) to ravage Cardigan and the vale of Towy, and his death is mentioned under 915. He was king of North Wales.

Ibid. Northumbrians. That is, the Northumbrian Danes, those who had occupied Northumbria under Halfdene (cp. *supra*, p. 33, 35, and notes).

Page 63. *Leonaford.* This place has not been identified.

Ibid. Congresbury. According to tradition this place was given by Ine to Saint Congar, and a collegiate church was founded there for twelve canons in 711, but nothing is really known of this foundation (cp. *Monasticon*, VI. 1465).

Ibid. Banwell. "Leland (*Itin.*, VII. 105) says that there was a monastery there." The supposed site was that of the "bishop's palace." Nothing is known of this foundation (cp. *Monasticon*, VI. 1622). It may be mentioned that Amesbury has been suggested in place of Congresbury as the first of the two monasteries presented to Asser, but the historical house there dates from 980 at earliest (*Monasticon*, VI. 333).

Page 64. *Exeter.* For a discussion of this question, cp. Introduction, p. xix.

Ibid. How the pagans besieged Paris. This passage is based on that in the *Chronicle*, s. a. For the siege of Paris, which was defended by Odo, there is a minute but very difficult metrical account of the siege by Abbo, who was an eye-witness (Pertz, *Mon. Ger.*, II. 776 *et seq.*). Other details may be found in the *Chronicle* of Regino (*s. a.* 887).

Ibid. Thirty-fifth. This should be thirty-eighth (cp. *supra*, note to p. 37).

Ibid. Seine. It may be noted that Asser uses the Old English Signe (Sigene) for the Seine, in preference to the classical Sequana.

Page 65. *That city is built.* Cp. Introduction, p. xxvii.

Ibid. How Alfred restored London. This passage is based on the *Chronicle* (*s. a.* 886)—"In the same year King Alfred occupied (*al.* restored) London (*al.* the burh of London ; MS. A, Lunden burg ;

MS. E. Lunden burh ; MS. F, the burh Lundene), and turned all
the Angle-kin to him, except those who were in captivity to the
Danes, and he entrusted the town to Ethered (Ethelred) the ealdorman to hold." It would appear that London was left in the hands
of the Danes after the battle of Edington. A "siege" of London
by Alfred is recorded by Ethelwerd (517 A), but not in the *Chronicle*,
and he is possibly preserving an additional fact. It was perhaps the
direct result of the breach of the peace by the Danes of East
Anglia (cp. *supra*, p. 49) that London was recovered by Wessex.

Page 65. *Restored . . and made it habitable.* In the *Chronicle* the
word "gesette" is used, which is ambiguous, and can mean either
"restored" or "occupied" ; it is similar in its ambiguity to the
Elizabethan use of the word "to plant." There seems no reasonable doubt that Asser was aware of the ambiguity, and that he
wished to bring out both senses of the word, which he does in the
text. This would seem to be a more reasonable view than that he
merely deduced the fact that London had to be restored before it
could be inhabited or re-garrisoned (as Stevenson suggests, *op.
cit.*, p. 324). On the other hand, there is every possibility that
London may have suffered very severely in the sack recorded in 851
(cp. *supra*, p. 4).

Ibid. Who had been in captivity with the pagans. This is apparently
a misunderstanding of the statement of the *Chronicle* (cp. above).
It is, however, possible that many English left the part of England
which was under Danish rule and took up their residence in Wessex.
This would have been the natural result of the recovery of Wessex
under Alfred.

Ibid. Concerning Grimbald and the men of Oxford. For this forgery,
cp. Introduction, p. xlvii.

Page 67. *How the pagans warred in the land of the West Franks.*
This passage and that which follows are based on the *Chronicle*, s. a.
887.

Ibid. Thirty-sixth. This should be thirty-ninth (cp. note to
p. 37).

Ibid. Left the city of Paris. Cp. Regino (*Chronicle* s. a. 887, 888).

Page 68. *Charles, king of the Franks.* Charles III. died on January
12, 888. He is called " Farlus " in this passage in the text.

Ibid. Arnulf. He was a bastard son of Carloman (for whom cp.

supra, note to p. 48), the eldest son of Lewis the German. This Carloman is to be distinguished from his cousin, who was killed by the boar (cp. p. 47).

Page 68. *Had driven him from that kingdom.* Cp. Regino (*s. a.* 887). At a council held on November 11, 887, Charles was deposed on the ground that he was physically and mentally incapable of government. The immediate cause of his deposition was, no doubt, his failure to relieve Paris ; he arrived there with an army, but as the chronicler says, "there did he nothing worthy of imperial majesty."

Ibid. Five kings were ordained. This is not strictly accurate ; the dismemberment of the empire had begun before the death of Charles. Asser also omits the kingdom of Boso, Provence, which had been created in 879, and which passed to Lewis, Boso's son, on his death in January 887.

Ibid. The other four kings, etc. This is quite accurate. Some sort of supremacy seems to have been conceded to Arnulf, though he did not assume the imperial title until 896. He was king of the East Franks from 887 to 899.

Ibid. Rudolf. King of Burgundy, 888–911. He was the son of Conrad, nephew of Judith, the wife of Lewis the Pious.

Ibid. Odo. King of the West Franks, 888–898. He was the son of Robert the Strong, count of France, the ancestor of the Capetian dynasty, and probably owed his election to his great defence of Paris against the Normans. The hereditary heir was Charles the Simple, son of Lewis II, who eventually succeeded Odo.

Ibid. Berengar. King of Italy, 887–924 ; emperor, 915. He was the son of Eberhard, marquis of Friuli, and of Gisela, sister of Charles the Bald.

Ibid. Guido. Guido, or Wido, king of Italy (in opposition to Berengar), 888-896 ; emperor, 896-899. He was the son of Guido, count of Spoleto, and of Rothilda, daughter of Lothar I. At first he tried to secure the succession in West Francia, but though he was crowned at Langres, he retired shortly to Italy, and there disputed the title of Berengar.

Page 69. *How Alfred sent alms to Rome.* To the passage in the *Chronicle* (*s. a.* 887) Asser adds that Ethelhelm was ealdorman of Wiltshire. From the *Chronicle* it is clear that there were almost annual missions to Rome (cp. *s. a.* 888, 890 ; and the notice under 889 that in that year no alms were sent to Rome).

Page 69. *To read*. That is, to read Latin. Cp. *supra*, note to p. 19, and Introduction, p. xxii.

Page 70. *A little book*. Cp. *supra*, p. 19 and notes.

Page 71. *That happy thief*. Luke xxiii. 39–43.

Page 72. *Enchiridion*. The Handbook would appear to have been still extant in the time of William of Malmesbury, who quotes it in his *Life of Aldhelm* (*Gest. Pont.*, ed. Hamilton, R. S., p. 333–336). The name was, perhaps, borrowed from Saint Augustine's *Enchiridion de Fide*, where the meaning of the word is carefully explained (*En. de Fide*, chap. 4 *et seq.* ; Migne, Pat. Lat., Vol. XL., col. 232 *et seq.*).

Ibid. Wakeful are the minds, etc. The source of this quotation is unknown.

Page 73. *No rest even for a single hour*. This would seem to be an exaggeration (cp. *supra*, note to p. 50). The following statement as to Alfred's despair is also probably not to be taken literally, it is inconsistent with the previous statement that he was naturally merry (cp. *supra*, p. 54).

Ibid. Concerning the glory of Alfred. This passage is paralleled in Einhard, (*Vit. Kar. Mag.*, c. 16).

Ibid. Ireland. There is some doubt whether "Hiberniae " or " Iberiae " should be read here.

Ibid. Elias. Elias III, patriarch of Jerusalem, 879–907. The text has Abel, but no such patriarch is known at this period. Plummer (*op. cit.*, p. 33–34) has suggested that " Abel " has been written for " ab El(ia)," and this suggestion has been here adopted. As Plummer points out, Abel makes hopeless Latin, as there is no preposition. He quotes from *Cockayne's Leechdoms*, a notice of certain recipes sent to Alfred by Elias, patriarch of Jerusalem (*Cockayne*, ii. 291). The recipes in question were concerned with the uses of balsam, triacle, and white stone (*ibid.*, ii. 289).

Ibid. Work in gold and silver. The word "aedificia " is here used in conjunction with "gold and silver," which argues in favour of Plummer's suggested rendering of "aedificia " (cp. *supra*, note to p. 43).

Page 75. *Fortresses . . . which have not been begun*, etc. It may perhaps be suggested that the rapid success of the second Danish invasion under Sweyn and Canute was partially due to the failure of the Saxons to carry out the project for the defence of their country by means of "burhs." For the work of Alfred in constructing "burhs," to which the people might retire for refuge when the Danes came, cp. Oman, *Art of War* (p. 110–111). The same system was adopted by Charles the Bald, and at a later date by Henry the Fowler. It is paralleled by the defensive system created by the Heraclian and Isaurian dynasties as a defence against the Saracens.

Page 75. *I call repentance vain.* The allusion is, perhaps, to Gen. xxiv. 34–38 ; cp. Heb. xii. 17 ; and to 2 Cor. vii. 9–10.

Page 76. *Concerning the monastery of Athelney.* Alleged to have been founded as a result of the vision of Saint Cuthbert. (Will. Malm., *Gest. Reg.*, I. 126 ; *Gest. Pont.*, p. 199.) Date of foundation is said to have been 888, and its alleged endowment ten "cassates" of land. (Cp. Will. Malm., *Gest. Pont.*, loc. cit., *Monasticon*, II. 402 *et seq.*, ed. 1844.)

Ibid. Causeways. "Cauticis" : wrongly emended to "nauticis" in the text : cp. Plummer (*op. cit.*, p. 25).

Page 77. *The desire for the monastic life.* For the decayed condition of monasticism in England, prior to the reforms of Dunstan, cp. Stubbs, *Mem. of Saint Dunstan* (Introduction, p. xcvii *et seq.*).

Page 78. *How there was a plot,* etc. The mistaken idea that John the Old Saxon is said by Asser to have been murdered on this occasion has been made the basis of attacks on the authenticity of the *Life*.

Page 79. *The last error shall be worse than the first.* Matt. xxvi. 64.

Page 81. *How the king founded a nunnery at Shaftesbury.* The alleged date of the foundation is 888 : possibly in this case, and in that of Athelney, the date is a mere deduction from the order of events in Asser. Endowed with a hundred hides, and dedicated to the Virgin. Its foundation has been ascribed to other persons than Alfred. (*Monasticon*, II. 471 *et seq.*, ed. 1844.)

Page 82. *If thou offerest rightly,* etc. Gen. iv. 7, the version being the old version made from the Septuagint, and not the Vulgate.

Ibid. The king's heart, etc. Prov. xxi. 1.

Ibid. How he provided for the king's service. For the similar military reforms of Alfred, see Oman, *Art of War*, p. 108 ff.

Page 84. *God loveth a cheerful giver.* 2 Cor. ix. 7.

Page 84. *Give not little*, etc. This is a misquotation of Gregory the Great, *Pastoral Care*, iii. 21 (cp. Works, ed. Rome, 1591, Vol. III, p. 183 C) : the passage there reading, "And it is therefore needful that they labour diligently that they may not distribute these things that are entrusted to them unworthily ; that they may not distribute something to those to whom they should distribute nothing, or nothing to those to whom something is due, or much to those to whom little, or little to those to whom much," etc. It may be noted that in Alfred's version of the *Pastoral Care* the passage is rendered rightly (cp. ed. Sweet, *E. E. T. S.*, p. 321), so that it seems likely that Asser was here trying to quote from memory.

Page 85. *Those serving God*, etc. Cp. Einhard, *Vit. Kar. Mag.*, c. 27. For the generosity of Charles to the poor, cp. *ibid.*, c. 27.

Ibid. Sometimes even in Ireland. It will be noticed that Asser does not mention the mission of Alfred to India, which appears in the *Chronicle*, s. a. 883, MS. E. Gibbon (*Decline and Fall*, c. xlvii ; ed. Bury, Vol. V. 151, and note 126) remarks, "I almost suspect that the English ambassadors collected their cargo and legend in Egypt." The marvellous character of the story also appeared to William of Malmesbury (*Gest. Reg.*, I. 130). In the present passage it will be noted that Asser considered it remarkable that Alfred should concern himself with the welfare of the Irish monasteries, and it is curious that the sending of alms to India should not have struck him as still more remarkable. It would seem at least possible that the suggestion of Gibbon is correct, if indeed the whole story is not an exaggeration. In any case it does not seem to be fair to attack the authenticity of Asser on the score that he does not mention the Indian mission (cp. Stevenson, *op. cit.*, p. 288 *et seq.*).

Ibid. Whosoever would give, etc. This quotation is really drawn from Saint Augustine, *Enchiridion de Fide*, c. 76 (Migne, Pat. Lat., Vol. 40, col. 268).

Page 91. *Now we have set forth*, etc. As to the abrupt ending of the *Life*, cp. Introduction, p. xxii. For the interpolations here added by Parker, cp. notes on interpolations, p. 150.

II. On the Interpolations.

Page 4. *And the city of London.* For the retention of this addition from the *Annals of Saint Neot*, cp. *supra*, note to p. 4.

Page 5. *Ethelwulf, king of the West Saxons.* The MS., according to Wise, whose statements are throughout quoted, omitted the word "West," which is, however, retained from *Florence of Worcester* as being in conformity with the terminology of the rest of the *Life*.

Ibid. Athelstan the king. "Son of King Ethelwulf" has been added from the *Annals*, but it is more probable that Athelstan was really the son of Egbert (cp. *supra*, note to p. 5).

Page 6. *The Lord Pope Leo.* His numeral "IV" has been added from the *Annals*; it does not appear in the MS.

Page 7. *And concerning Edmund*, etc. This passage is added from the *Annals of Saint Neot*, it is not found in *Florence of Worcester* or in the *Chronicle*. According to the legend, Edmund was born in 841, succeeded, in 855, the childless King Offa of East Anglia, to whom his good qualities had appealed, was crowned in 856, and fixed his residence at Bures (cp. Arnold, *Mem. of St. Edmund's Abbey*, Introduction, xv *et seq.*, and Abbo, *Passio Sancti Eadmundi, passim*, Mem., I. 6–25). (Cp. also note to p. 24.)

Ibid. Lothar. Lothar I, son of Lewis the Pious, and brother of Charles the Bald; emperor 840–855.

Ibid. Lewis, the most pious Augustus. Lewis the Pious, son of Charles the Great; emperor 814–840.

Ibid. Charles III, son of Lewis II. This is Charles the Fat, son of Lewis the German, for whom cp. *supra*, note to p. 48. It is an error to describe the year 855 as the first of the Emperor Charles III, who did not receive the imperial title until 881.

Page 8. *King Ethelbald.* "Son of King Ethelwulf" has been added from the *Annals*.

Page 12. *Dwell among the Saxons.* "West" is added before Saxons in the *Annals of Saint Neot*.

Ibid. Charles, king of the Franks. The epithets "great" and "most famous" appear in the *Annals*, and the latter is retained in *Florence of Worcester*.

Page 15. *When King Ethelwulf was dead.* " And was buried at Steyning " is added by the *Annals ;* "and was buried at Winchester " is added, rightly, by *Florence of Worcester* (cp. *Chronicle,* s. a. 855).

Ibid. How Edmund was made king of the East Angles. This passage is interpolated from the *Annals of Saint Neot.*

Ibid. Second year of the Emperor Charles III. This is not correct (cp. *supra,* note to interpolation on p. 7).

Ibid. Humbert. Bishop of Elmham ; he is said to have been consecrated about 826 (*Monasticon,* IV, 1, note *a* ; ed. 1844). In the *St. Albans Chronicle* (Matt. Paris, *Chron. Maj.,* I. 396) he appears as the bishop whom Edmund consulted on the eve of his martyrdom, and who advised submission to Ingwar. The story is found in Abbo (*op. cit.,* Arnold, *Mem.* I. 11–15), where, however, no name is given.

Page 16. *Bures.* Burua in the text. This is an error for Burun, which is given as the residence of Edmund in Geoffrey de Fontibus, *De Infantia Sancti Eadmundi* (Arnold, *Mem.* I. 101), and which is identified with Bures St. Mary, on the border of Suffolk and Essex.

Ibid. Ethelbald. " King of the West Saxons " has been added from the *Annals.*

Page 21. *Almost all the Northumbrians. Florence* inserts " host of the."

Ibid. The two kings. The *Annals* add " with many nobles."

Page 22. *Birth of King Alfred.* The *Annals* add " there was a great famine."

Page 23. *And Alfred.* These words are supplied from *Florence.*

Ibid. Twenty-first from the birth of King Alfred. The *Annals* continue, " there was a great famine, and mortality among men, and a pestilence among the beasts. And," etc.

Page 25. *King Ethelred.* The *Annals* add, " of the West Saxons."

Ibid. But, alas. The *Annals* insert " heu," in addition to the " proh dolor."

Page 26. *They likewise.* " Likewise " has been retained from the *Annals.*

Ibid. Depart thence alive. " Alive " has been retained from the *Annals.*

Page 33. *Thegn of the king.* "Of the king" has been retained from the *Annals.*

Page 34. *And Trent.* The name of the second river has been supplied from *Florence.*

Ibid. Upon all the relics. The *Annals* add, "And on the ring on which," etc. (they had never before sworn). Cp. *supra*, note to p. 34.

Ibid. All the horsemen. For the addition of " rex " here by *Florence* cp. *supra*, note to p. 34.

Ibid. Civitas Exae. "Exae" is added by Florence, and here retained.

Page 35. *How Rollo*, etc. This passage comes from the *Annals*, as will be seen in the text. There we have also an account of the dream of Rollo. Rollo, more properly Hrolf, is, of course, the founder of the duchy of Normandy, that district being granted to him by Charles the Simple, by the treaty of St. Clair-sur-Epte (*circa* 911).

Ibid. How Alfred caused ships, etc. This passage was not to be found in the MS. (according to Wise), and has been added from the *Annals.* It is a somewhat confused and slightly enhanced duplicate of the passage already given above (p. 34). On the other hand, it is clearly based on the *Chronicle* (*s. a.* 877). The details as to the orders given to the fleet are realistic and sound plausible.

Page 36. *Pirates.* Probably Frisians. There is an interesting parallel in the "robber legion" of Henry the Fowler, for which cp. Widukind, *Res. Gest. Sax.*, II. 3.

Ibid. Some on horseback, some in ships. This supplies the true version of the obscure passage above (p. 34), cp. *supra*, note to p. 34.

Page 38. *The story of the burning of the cakes.* This passage is from the *Annals of Saint Neot* (cp. Introduction, p. xlvi).

Ibid. "Ah, you man," etc. The following rendering of this passage occurs in Dr. Giles' translation (quoted by Gairdner, *Early Chroniclers of Europe : England*, p. 37)—

"Ca'sn thee mind the ke-aks, man, and doossen zee 'em burn ?
I'm boun thee's eat 'em vast enough, az zoon az 'tiz the turn."

This would appear to be an excellent rendering of the Somersetshire dialect, though perhaps neither "eat" nor "enough" is quite true to the district.

Page 38. *How Alfred merited his misfortunes.* This probably libellous passage is from the *Annals.* As to the character given to Alfred in these and similar interpolations, cp. Introduction, p. xlix.

Page 39. *Neot.* The legendary *Life of Saint Neot* says that he was admitted as a monk at Glastonbury in 850, being of the royal house of Wessex, and became sacristan there. In this position he acquired a great reputation, and to escape the consequences of his popularity retired to Cornwall, and to a place called then Ham-stoke, where there was a chapel to Saint Gueryr. Here for a while he lived the life of a hermit ; but, having visited Rome, the pope persuaded him to abandon his solitary life. On his return, he founded a monastery at Ham-stoke, which acquired the name of Neot-stoke, preserved in St. Neots, near Liskeard. He died there in 877, and was buried in the chapel of Saint Gueryr. About a century later his relics were stolen and carried to St. Neots in Huntingdonshire, where a monastery was founded in his honour (*Mon.*, III. 460 *et seq.*, ed. 1844). His holy well is still to be seen at St. Neots in Cornwall, and a legend of his fish is preserved. For the identification of Saint Neot with Athelstan, sub-king of Kent, which was worked out by Whittaker and incorporated in the "Life of Saint Neot" in *Tracts for the Times*, cp. *supra*, note to p. 5.

Page 40. *By the siege.* This is retained from the *Annals.*

Page 41. *How the Raven Banner was taken.* This passage is from the *Annals.* A notice of the capture of the banner here is found in the *Chronicle*, MS. E (*s. a.* 878) (cp. Earle and Plummer, *op. cit.*, II. 93, where there is another version of the legend, quoted from the *Gesta Cnutonis*).

Ibid. A few men. The *Annals* substitute "helpers" for "men."

Ibid. Chief men. The *Annals* add "vassals."

Ibid. Somerset. The *Annals* add "district"—"of the district of Somerset," and also supply "contra" to follow the "rebellavit" of the text.

Page 43. *After seven weeks.* The number is supplied from *Florence*, probably incorrectly (cp. *supra*, note to p. 43).

Page 44. *Ghent.* The place-name is from the *Annals.*

Page 48. *Armorica.* The *Annals* add, " that is, Lesser Britain."

Page 48. *Son of Charles.* In the text of the MS., Lewis was made the son of Pippin ; the correct descent is supplied from the *Annals.*

Page 50. *Concerning the earlier illnesses of Alfred.* For the reasons for regarding this passage as interpolated, cp. *supra*, note to p. 50.

Ibid. Saint Gueryr. Nothing is recorded of this saint.

Ibid. Saint Neot. Cp. *supra*, note to interpolation on p. 39.

Page 51. *For he feared leprosy,* etc. It will be noted that leprosy and blindness are here regarded as lighter afflictions than the "ficus," which seems to be absurd.

Page 52. *Edmund.* The lacuna here is supplied from Rudborne by Wise (cp. *M. H. B.*, Asser, p. 485, note *a*).

Page 65. *Concerning Grimbald,* etc. For a note on this forgery, cp. *supra*, Introduction, p. xlvii.

Page 66. *Gildas.* Flourished *circa* 550, author of the *Liber Querulus*, "the Groans of the Britons."

Ibid. Nennius. Flourished *circa* 796; author of the *Historia Britonum.*

Ibid. Kentigern (St. Mungo). The apostle of Strathclyde : flourished *circa* 518–603.

Ibid. Germanus. St. Germanus, bishop of Auxerre, flourished 380–448. His mission to Britain is described in Bede, I. 17–21.

Page 67. *Saint Peter.* The present church of St. Peter-in-the-East, which contains the so-called "Grimbald's crypt," which dates from the eleventh century.

Page 68. *That realm divided.* "Divisio fuit" is retained from the *Annals.*

Page 91. *Ad finem.* Parker, in his edition, here added a notice of the death of Alfred, from the *Annals*, the metrical panegyric on Alfred, which is found in *Henry of Huntingdon* (ed. Arnold, p. 152), and a notice of the death of Asser.

TABLE OF DATES

A.D.

855. Second visit of Alfred to Rome, where he and Ethelwulf
     remain a whole year; restoration of the School of the
     Saxons.

     The Danes winter in Thanet.

     Ethelwulf marries Judith, daughter of Charles the Bald, at
     Verberie, Oct. 15.

     Conspiracy of Ethelbald; partition of Wessex; Ethelwulf
     receives Kent.

858. Death of Ethelwulf (Jan. 13); Ethelbald reigns in Wessex;
     Ethelbert in Kent.

     Ethelbald marries his step-mother, Judith.

860. Death of Ethelbald; reunion of the kingdom under
     Ethelbert.

     Sack of Winchester by the Danes, who are then defeated by
     the ealdormen of Hampshire and Berkshire.

862. Judith elopes with Baldwin, count of Flanders, to whom she
     is married in the following year.

863. Osbert, king of Northumbria, is expelled by Ella, who becomes
     king.

864. The Danes winter in Thanet; attempt of the men of Kent
     to buy off the Danes; eastern Kent ravaged.

866. Death of Ethelbert; accession of Ethelred.

     Danish invasion of East Anglia.

867. Danish invasion of Northumbria; Osbert and Ella unite
     their forces against them, but are defeated and slain at
     York.

     Death of Eahlstan, bishop of Sherborne.

868. Alfred marries Elswitha, daughter of Ethelred, ealdorman of
     the Gaini.

     Alfred and Ethelred go to the assistance of Burhred against
     the Danes, they reach Nottingham, but fail to force a
     battle.

869. Second Danish invasion of Northumbria.

870. Second Danish invasion of East Anglia; martyrdom of Saint
     Edmund after the battle of Hoxne (Nov. 30).

     Death of Ceolnoth, archbishop of Canterbury.

871. Danish invasion of Wessex.

A.D.

The Danes form a fortified camp at Reading.

Battle of Englefield ; the Danes defeated by Ethelwulf, ealdorman of Berkshire.

Battle of Reading ; Ethelred and Alfred defeated.

Battle of Ashdown ; victory of Ethelred and Alfred.

Battle of Basing ; defeat of Ethelred and Alfred.

Battle of Mertun ; defeat of Ethelred and Alfred.

Death of Ethelred ; accession of Alfred.

? Second battle of Reading ; defeat of Alfred.

Battle of Wilton ; defeat of Alfred.

872. The Danes occupy London.

873. Death of Nobis, bishop of St. David's.

The Danes in Northumbria.

Werferth, bishop of Worcester.

874. The Danes at Repton ; Burhred driven from his kingdom ; Ceowulf set up as a puppet king.

875. Division of the Danish army ; Halfdene occupies Northumbria ; Guthrum at Cambridge.

Naval victory of Alfred.

876. Death of Rhodri Mawr ; accession of Anaraut in Gwynedd.

Settlement of Northumbria by the Danes under Halfdene.

Mercia divided by the Danes ; Ceowulf retains part.

The Danes occupy Wareham.

The Danes besiege Exeter.

Naval victory of the Saxons at Swanage.

Charles the Fat becomes king of Alamannia.

877. Death of Charles the Bald ; accession of Lewis II.

878. The Danes occupy Chippenham, and begin the second invasion of Wessex.

Alfred takes refuge at Athelney, which he fortifies.

The Danes ravage South Wales.

Defeat of the Danes at Cynwit by Odda.

Battle of Edington ; Alfred defeats the Danes.

Treaty of Wedmore ; baptism of Guthrum (Guthrum-Athelstan).

The Danes evacuate Wessex.

879. Death of Lewis II ; accession of Lewis III and Carloman.

A.D.

Charles the Fat becomes king of Italy.

The Danes at Cirencester.

A second Danish army at Fulham.

880. The Danes retire to East Anglia, which they settle.

The second Danish army goes to Ghent.

Charles the Fat becomes king of Bavaria.

881. Battle of Saucourt; the Danes defeated by Lewis III.

882. Naval victory of Alfred.

Death of Lewis III; Carloman sole king of West Franks.

884. Danish attack on Rochester repulsed.

The East Anglian Danes break the peace; naval expedition against them defeated at the mouth of the Stour.

Death of Pope Marinus I.

Death of Carloman; Charles the Fat sole king of the Franks.

884 or 885 (?). Asser first comes to Alfred.

885 (?). Asser's illness; his second visit to Alfred.

886. Siege of Paris by the Northmen.

Alfred restores London.

887. Siege of Paris raised.

Deposition of Charles the Fat; disruption of the Frankish empire.

Alfred sends alms to Rome.

888. Death of Charles the Fat.

Death of Ethelswitha, widow of Burhred of Mercia.

890. Death of Guthrum-Athelstan.

Plegmund becomes archbishop of Canterbury.

892. Renewal of the Danish attacks on Wessex.

Death of Hemeid, king of Dyfed.

893. Asser writes his *Life of Alfred*.

896. End of the Danish invasions.

901 (?). Death of Alfred; accession of Edward the Elder.

903. Death of Saint Grimbald.

905. Death of Elswitha, widow of Alfred.

906, or 908, or 910. Death of Asser.

GENEALOGICAL TABLE

(To illustrate *The Life of Alfred*)

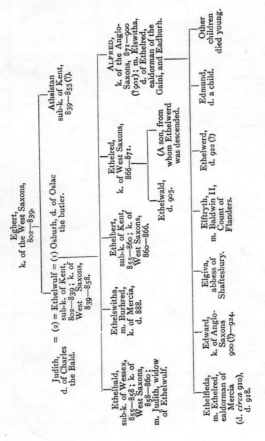

Egbert, k. of the West Saxons, 802—839.

Judith, d. of Charles the Bald. = (2) = Ethelwulf = (1) Osburh, d. of Oslac the butler.
sub-k. of Kent, 802—839; k. of West Saxons, 839—858.

Athelstan sub-k. of Kent, 839—855 (?).

Ethelbald, sub-k. of Wessex, 855—858; k. of West Saxons, 858—860; m. Judith, widow of Ethelwulf.

Ethelswitha, m. Burhred, k. of Mercia, d. 888.

Ethelbert, sub-k. of Kent, 855—860; k. of West Saxons, 860—866.

Ethelred, k. of West Saxons, 866—871.

ALFRED, k. of the Anglo-Saxons, 871—900 (?901); m. Elswitha, d. of Ethelred, ealdorman of the Gaini, and Eadburh.

Ethelwald, d. 905.

(A son, from whom Ethelwerd was descended.)

Ethelfleda, m. Ethelred, ealdorman of Mercia (d. *circa* 910), d. 918.

Edward, k. of Anglo-Saxons 900 (?)—924.

Elgiva, abbess of Shaftesbury.

Elfryth, m. Baldwin II, Count of Flanders.

Ethelwerd, d. 922 (?)

Edmund, d. a child.

Other children died young.

INDEX

Names which occur only in the interpolated passages are printed in italics